D0563012

# ALWAYS ON STRIKE

# Always on Strike

## FRANK LITTLE
## AND THE WESTERN WOBBLIES

Arnold Stead

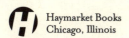

Haymarket Books
Chicago, Illinois

© 2014 Arnold Stead

Haymarket Books
PO Box 180165
Chicago, IL 60618
773-583-7884
info@haymarketbooks.org
www.haymarketbooks.org

ISBN: 978-1-60846-220-9

Trade distribution:
In the US, through Consortium Book Sales and Distribution, www.cbsd.com
In Canada, Publishers Group Canada, www.pgcbooks.ca
In the UK, Turnaround Publisher Services, www.turnaround-uk.com
All other countries, Publishers Group Worldwide, www.pgw.com

Special discounts are available for bulk purchases by organizations and institutions.
Please contact Haymarket Books for more information at 773-583-7884
or info@haymarketbooks.org.

This book was published with the generous support of Lannan Foundation and the
Wallace Action Fund.

Cover design by Julie Fain.

Library of Congress Cataloging-in-Publication Data is available.

Printed in Canada by union labor.

10 9 8 7 6 5 4 3 2 1

RECYCLED
Paper made from
recycled material
FSC® C103567

*To the memory of my brother, Christopher Anthony Stead,*
*a workingman and artist*

# CONTENTS

# INTRODUCTION

Many years after the fact, during a far more conservative period of his life, Ralph Chaplin writes that Frank Little was the first to arrive for a meeting of the General Executive Board of the Industrial Workers of the World in late July of 1917. Although we may have reason to doubt his memory (it has Little leaving Chicago en route to Butte a full week after that city's press announced the hobo agitator's arrival in Montana), Chaplin's vivid description of his last encounter with Little has a ring of truth to it. He writes: "Frank wore his Stetson at the same jaunty angle, and his twisted grin was as aggressive as ever." The meeting's primary purpose was to decide whether or not Wobblies should register for the draft. Board member Richard Brazier, like Chaplin and Haywood, thought opposing conscription would put the International Workers of the World, known as the IWW or the Wobblies, "out of business." Little shot back at him: "They'll run us out of business anyhow. Better to go out in a blaze of glory than to give in. Either we're for this capitalist slaughter fest or we're against it. I'd rather take a firing squad."

In response, "Bill [Haywood] looked angry, the others bewildered," and Chaplin hastily wrote a "compromise statement." The board would not sign it, but instead told Chaplin to send it under his signature. He remembers taking the statement with him when he registered for the draft. The following day, July 25, Chaplin writes that Little "hobbled up to my offices to say goodbye." The latter said, "You're wrong about registering for the draft. It would be better to go down slugging." Chaplin "marveled" at Little's "courage in taking on a difficult and dangerous assignment like [the Butte strike] in his present condition." Chaplin continues:

"'It's a fine specimen the I.W.W. is sending into that tough town,' I chided him. 'One leg, one eye, two crutches—and no brains!'

Frank laughed, he lifted a crutch as though to crown me. 'Don't worry, fellow worker, all we're going to need from now on is guts.'

That was the last time I saw Frank Little alive."

Historian Arnon Gutfeld describes the assassination of Frank Little: At about three a.m. the morning of August 1, "a large black car stopped in front of 316 North Wyoming Street." Six masked men emerged from the vehicle and entered a boarding house next to Finnlander Hall where Frank Little was staying. The men frightened the landlady, Mrs. Nora Byrne, by kicking in the door of a room they mistakenly thought Little to be occupying. She asked them what they wanted and they replied, "We are officers and we want Frank Little." His abductors did not allow the hobo agitator to dress, and when he resisted they carried him to the black automobile.

"The car sped away, but stopped after traveling a short distance and Little, still in his underwear, was tied to the car bumper.

He must have been dragged a considerable distance, for his kneecaps were later found to have been scrapped off. He was taken to the Milwaukee Bridge, a short distance outside the city limits. There he was severely beaten, as bruises on his skull indicated, and hanged from a railroad trestle. Pinned to his underwear was a six-by-ten inch placard with the inscription, 'Others take notice, first and last warning, 3-7-77.' On the bottom of the note, the letters 'L-D-C-S-S-W-T' were printed, and the letter 'L' encircled."

The numbers 3–7-77 aroused a good many theories, including one by a Butte citizen who believed it was Little's draft number and that he committed suicide to avoid being inducted into the military. It is now generally believed, however, that the figures designate Montana specifications for a grave: three feet wide, seven feet deep, and seventy-seven inches long. The Butte press seemed to think D-C-S-S-W-T stood for the last names of men the "vigilantes" were going to "visit" next: William Dunne, Tom Campbell, Joe Shannon, Dan Shovlin, John Williams, and Leon Tomich; "all of whom were leaders of the Metal Mine Workers Union."

◆

I first discovered Frank Little quite by accident. With no students to occupy me during office hours, I began to browse through the *Encyclopedia of the American Left* and found in an entry on the great novelist Dashiell Hammett that some people believed he had been involved in the lynching of Frank Little. Long a Hammett fan, I had never heard of Frank Little. Under the former's name I found a fragment of a thought-provoking figure, and I have been collecting Frank Little fragments ever since. If not for my interest in Dashiell Hammett, creator of characters such as Sam Spade and Nick and Nora Charles, I might well have never discovered Frank Little, a legendary figure in his own right. Hammett would have been about twenty-one years old when Little was murdered and highly unlikely to have had any notions of one day being a respected writer of hard-boiled detective fiction.

Young Hammett was working as a Pinkerton operative in Butte, Montana, the summer Frank Little was murdered.[1] He was in town to help break the miners' strike that Little was probably leading, clandestinely of course. In those days, the agency that Alan Pinkerton had founded at the behest of the nation's biggest bosses, particularly the railroad magnates, did its bread-and-butter business as a strike-breaking force. The Industrial Workers of the World was involved in a strike against the Butte branch of the Anaconda Copper Company so the company hired Pinkertons. According to William F. Nolan, one of Hammett's biographers, "Hammett discovered that one man in particular was causing major trouble for the mining company. His name was Frank Little, a labor union organizer known as the 'hobo agitator.' Little, who had lost one eye, was part Indian and possessed a warrior's tenacity and courage; he would not be bluffed or scared off. Union members supported him enthusiastically as he raved and shouted against injustices in the mines." Might we assume the man who could not be "bluffed or scared off" had to be killed?

In the early 1930s, Hammett told Lillian Hellman that an officer of Anaconda Copper had offered him five thousand dollars to kill Frank Little. He also said: "I had no political conscience in '17. I was just doing a job, and if our clients were rotten it didn't concern me. They hired us to break up a union strike, so we went out there [Butte] to do that." Hammett said he turned down the offer, but Hellman seems convinced the incident played a pivotal role in his life. In *Scoundrel Time* she tells her readers: "Through the years he was to repeat that bribe offer so many times, that I came to believe, knowing him now, that it was a kind of key to his life. He had given a man the right to think he would murder . . . I think I can date Hammett's belief that he was living in a corrupt society from Little's murder."

Hammett did not meet Hellman until approximately fifteen years after Little was lynched, yet Hammett could not put what happened in Butte behind him. Moreover, he spoke of the offer several times over the course of the couple's relationship. One cannot help but wonder if Hammett, in fact, did not refuse the offer. Or, perhaps he blamed himself for not doing something to prevent the assassination he knew was in the making.

Another of Hammett's biographers, Diane Johnson, writes that the author of *The Maltese Falcon* was raised by a hard-luck father with big ideas and little else. As a young man he was essentially conservative but had a penchant for seeking the company of grafters, gamblers, and sporting women. Like Hellman, Johnson speaks of the radical change in Hammett's life when she writes: "But at some moment—perhaps at the moment he was asked to murder Frank Little or perhaps at the moment he learned Little had been killed, possibly by Pinkerton men—Hammett saw that the actions of the guards and the guarded, of the detective and the man he's stalking, are reflexes of a single sensibility, on the fringe where murderers and thieves live. He saw that he himself was on the fringe, or might be."

Frank Little was neither thief nor murderer, but the Espionage Act took effect in June 1917 and made his criticism of the war and those fighting it a felony offense. While Little could not be described as a gunman, at the time of his death he may well have been carrying a gun. As early as 1913 he carried a pistol during a strike in Duluth, Minnesota, in order to ease the fears of his fellow strikers. The company's security forces were, of course, all packing a firearm or two. By the summer of 1917, with the United States now officially a combatant in the war, tensions were running significantly higher than they had been in Duluth; so carrying a firearm probably seemed like a sensible practice for a "hobo agitator" engaged in the dissemination of recently criminalized ideas.

Yet another of Dashiell Hammett's biographers, Richard Layman, calls the story of the five thousand dollar offer "implausible." He writes: "Hammett's accounts of his days as a detective are always suspect, because he was writing accounts, describing his adventures in interviews, and telling friends stories about his past after he changed occupations. He was by then a writer with experience and a considerable interest in advertising." While Layman's point is certainly worth noting, it ignores two important specifics. First, and most importantly, Hammett did not speak of the Butte offer just a few times over a short period of time but rather on many occasions over a considerable length of time. Second, he repeated the story to his lover and confidante, Lillian Hellman, to whom he had no need to advertise; at least not for so long a period of time.

My quest for Frank Little continued with a Google search of his name and found fifteen pages of information, a portion of which was of questionable reliability. I then perused a dozen labor-centered histories in order to find an equal number of repetitious pages about him. Only a handful of historians mentioned him at all, and the majority of them limited their comments to brief and often grisly accounts of his death. I considered pairing Little with Randolph Bourne, or maybe Susan Sontag after her reaction in the *New Yorker* to the September 11 attacks, and discussing them as pariahs of different, yet not-so-different types. Both projects interested me but more because of Bourne or Sontag than Frank Little. I still did not know enough about him, what exactly he did and why, to have more than a fascination with him comparable to my feelings as a boy for Robin Hood.

As chance would have it, a long and avid interest in history gave me an opportunity to teach an American History survey course in a tribal and community college urban outreach program. Teaching that course helped convince me I had the right to practice the historian's craft. I feared my research skills were not up to the historian or the biographer's task, but I plunged in anyway. As a result, the reader may find my portrait of Frank Little excessively impressionistic and speculative. He/she may suspect me of finding in Frank Little what I wished to find. If such a suspicion is to some degree correct, I must ultimately defend myself by saying a similar case of "finding what one wishes to find" is at play in a significant portion of what is commonly referred to as "objective history." Perhaps the affliction comes with the territory. As a historian, I have sought to bring a reasonably fresh perspective to what I think I know about the subject, ask a good many questions, and hope at least some of them are useful to further discourse.

There is little known about Frank Little before he springs to life as an Arizona member of the Western Federation of Miners in 1900. He was born in Illinois in 1879 to W. H. Little, a Quaker physician, and his Cherokee wife. He had four siblings, two brothers, W. F. and Alonzo, and two sisters whose names are unknown to me, as is their mother's. When Frank was two years old his family moved to Ingalls, Oklahoma, near Yale in the predominately Native American eastern part of the (then) territory. These seemingly fundamental facts are anything but undisputed; even the year of his birth is not unanimously agreed upon. In its article on Little's death the New York *Call* says he was born in Fresno, California, while the rest of those sources that mention his birthplace locate it in Illinois. With the exception of historian Nigel Anthony Sellars, they have him coming to Oklahoma at age two. According to Sellars, the Little family moved to Payne County in the 1890s "[after] his [Frank's] older brother Alonzo had staked a claim in the 1889 Land Run." If Sellars is correct, Little was approaching puberty when he arrived in Oklahoma. His father, W. H., is unanimously identified as a Quaker, but information about his mother's origins is far less certain. Marxist historian Philip S. Foner claims she was a full-blooded Cherokee while historian Melvyn Dubofsky says she was half Native American, and Nigel Sellars asserts that she was one-eighth Native American. He also says Frank "briefly attended Oklahoma Agricultural and Mechanical College in Stillwater." Writer Gene Lantz's timeline of Little's life places his brothers in college at Stillwater, but makes no mention of Frank ever attending. The New York *Call* reported that, until his death, Frank Little was the sole support of his mother and one of his sisters. Lantz writes that, as a young man, Little chewed tobacco and later in life suffered from rheumatism. The rest of what we know about Frank Little is found in what he did, said, and wrote as a Wobbly of the western variety. He showed himself to be proficient at transforming workingmen's quiet desperation into direct action. He wished others to step over the line drawn by the bosses and endure the punishment meted out for doing so; therefore, he must step over that line and suffer the consequences of his act. When enough workers followed his lead, the time for enduring punishment would end, and workers would show the guys "handy with a sap" what they could do. It would appear they intended to be on the giving rather than the receiving end of violence.

Violet Gilbert Snell's poem, "To Frank Little," speaks of his enemies referring to Little as "a wanton breeder of discontent," which could be interpreted as one who rouses the docile to action. He might more fittingly be called a lightning rod of discontent. The living conditions of those he sought to arouse make it easy enough to believe they were already a bubbling pot, but without a focus until men like Frank Little came along.

In making decisions about Little's movements one question repeatedly presented itself: Did a particular action focus on issues of primary importance to Little objectives? My judgments on this question may at times be mistaken, but I have not willfully placed him at the scene of any event that is at odds with the mandates of time and space or his documented activities as an IWW operative. Moreover, I have attempted to speculate as little as possible on the movements of a man who has been described as one of the most elusive figures in American labor history.[2]

From 1905 to 1917 the Industrial Workers of the World was the most aggressive and uncompromising labor union in the United States. While its predominantly Marxist eastern branch was often enough criticized by the more so-called respectable trade unionists, the western Wobblies embodied a spirit feared and hated by "legitimate" union leaders like Samuel Gompers. The western IWW's infectious influence was so great that William Appleton Williams, in his *The Contours of American History*, believes Henry Ford's decision to institute the five-dollar workday was to a substantial degree brought about by Ford's fear of the IWW invading his factories.

In chapter one, "The Western Wobblies," I discuss the two IWWs—east and west—which are too often viewed as a single, monolithic union and consider Frank Little as a decidedly western Wobbly. In order to understand him we need to feel at home in his world: the Wild West of the twentieth century's first two decades and the bottom-dog workers who went into the mines, felled the trees, drilled the oil, and harvested the crops an ever-hungry United States needed. The charge of violence was habitually laid at the door of the western IWW. In addressing this charge I draw on Georges Sorel, Walter Benjamin, and Hannah Arendt.

In his valuable little book, *Democracy*, Anthony Arblaster makes the following assertion: "Free debate, free choice, and genuine consent require . . . a level of education (which may not be formal education) in social understanding such that people are aware of themselves as the targets of persuasion and propaganda, and are thereby enabled to resist these pressures." Over a five-year period (1909–1914) the IWW took to the streets in an effort to make workers aware of themselves as "targets of persuasion and propaganda." Migratory workers were being swindled by employment agencies, so the IWW stepped in. Laws passed against the union's street meetings and 'soapbox speakers' forced the union to repeatedly fight for its right to address and educate the workers. Chapter two, "The Free-Speech Fights," discusses those struggles and Frank Little's substantial role in them. His last free-speech battle, his unshakable opposition to the United States entering World War One, brings to light the recurring and ever increasing tension between Little and Big Bill Haywood.

Chapter three, "Iron Miners, Harvest Hands, and Oil Workers," begins by chronicling and examining two miner strikes on the Mesabi Iron Range of Minnesota; one in 1913, the other in 1916. Frank Little led the first of those two strikes and participated in the second. The ore dockworkers' strike of 1913 has been all but lost to history. Little led this unsuccessful action, in which his advice came into public conflict with some of the striking workers. In 1916 he was one of the principal organizers of another large Iron Range strike. My discussion of the strikes makes considerable use of local newspaper accounts that, on both occasions, followed IWW activities quite closely throughout the iron range territory.

The Mesabi strikes served in part as opportunities to form an alliance between iron ore workers and harvest hands, a project in which Little was instrumental. The chapter offers a look at the forming of the Agricultural Workers Organization (AWO) and Little's germinal role in that undertaking. He likewise played an important role in spawning the Oil Workers Industrial Union (OWIU). These activities are chronicled and the tricky task Little faced in organizing oil workers is discussed.

The last year of any person's life takes on a certain weight by virtue of its finality, if nothing else. Frank Little's last year displays a clear consistency of principles and purpose brought to a fever pitch by World War One. The first half of chapter four, "Frank Little's Last Year," focuses on three events: a copper miners' strike in Butte, Montana; the "deportation" of more than eleven hundred workers in Bisbee, Arizona; and the "Green Corn Rebellion" in Oklahoma. Little was present at the first two and a notable influence on the third. His opposition to US involvement in the war abroad is also examined. Chapter four's second half, "One Hundred Sixty-Six Coconspirators," describes the government's nationwide raids on IWW offices, the arrest of various leaders, and the indictment of one hundred sixty-five Wobblies for conspiring with Frank H. Little to sabotage America's war effort. The subsequent conspiracy trial in Chicago involved over one hundred defendants and was the longest criminal trial in US history at the time. There were conspiracy trials in Sacramento and Wichita as well, but the focus here is on the Chicago proceedings.

I include two chapters that commence with an examination of Little's relationship to Big Bill Haywood, which, over a ten-year period, moved from adulation to rivalry to mistrust. This section also discusses the power exerted by the eastern establishment on America's cultural and intellectual ideals during Little and Haywood's time, as well as the ideological differences between the eastern IWW and the western branch, in order to better understand the two men's complex relationship.

Chapter six deals with Joe Hill, Frank Little, and Wesley Everest as western Wobbly martyrs. We see the East Coast financial-cultural establishment at work once again, this time helping make the troubadour Joe Hill a far better known historical figure than Little or Everest. The causes of this discrepancy are addressed and the motives behind it speculated upon.

The narrative's conclusion, "Frank Little, Where Are You When We Really Need You?," addresses the hobo agitator's relevance today.

*Always on Strike: Frank Little and the Western Wobblies* is little more than an introduction to its subject. If these pages inspire others to further research and serious consideration of the ideas and events they encounter here, the author will be well satisfied.

# CHAPTER ONE
# The Western Wobblies

The roots of the western Wobbly are found in the "placer miner," men who lived and worked in Utah, Nevada, Colorado, Montana, and Idaho during the latter half of the nineteenth century. He was a prospecting miner. His basic tool, a wash pan, allowed him to sample creek beds and other locations for precious metals. If he found something worth his trouble, he set to work building a "rocker" with hammer, nails, wire, other simple items he carried in his pack, and whatever wood he could find. Occasionally a placer miner struck it rich, like Marcus Daly, one of the founders of Anaconda Copper Company, who began as a prospector. Usually a placer miner made little more than a bare living, but he was his own man. Then the scent of money and cheap labor brought mining companies into the West. Melvyn Dubofsky speaks of industrial cities rapidly replacing frontier boom camps and heavily capitalized corporations striking up where placer miner/prospectors had been. With the arrival of the corporations, mining became a massive industrial undertakening, requiring railroads, milling and smelting facilities and a host of capital. By the time Frank Little was born (most sources say 1879 while a few others say 1880), many so-called frontier-mining settlements were anything but frontier.

Resentful and ready to rebel, the miners saw themselves as victims of an invasion by men with full bellies and soft hands, representatives of the real capitalists, who seldom came west and, when they did, were very unlikely to confront any miners face to face. These toadies of capitalist power smelled of cologne and threw around ten-dollar words as they might have pocket change. Condescending and sweet smelling, they had come to the West with dollar signs in their eyes. But let their swagger take them too far and a westerner with clenched fists and a dog-off-his-leash gleam in his eyes step too close to those condescending smirks and the swagger began to wobble at the knees, the voice suddenly cracked, and the face too often presented an obscenely frightened smile. That fear told the westerner somewhere, not so very deep inside, the easterner was empty. The invaders were on strange ground while the miners were at home, sure of their necessary place in the scheme of things, at the center of which was their independence and mining. I do not mention freedom because as one of the men might have told you: "If a man's got his independence, what he digs is his own and he goes his own way. And if that ain't freedom, I don't know what you'd call it. Working for wages is nothing but slavery without the whip."

A placer miner commonly wore a pistol on his hip as protection against bandits, renegades, claim jumpers, and wildcats. A few sticks of dynamite could be found in his pack. When he went into town for supplies, he often indulged in a bottle of whiskey and a woman, or a game of stud poker, or maybe a good old-fashioned brawl just to take the edge off. You have no doubt seen a version of the character I am describing in any number of western movies and television. *Gun Smoke's* Festus comes to mind. He might treat himself to clean sheets, a hot bath, and a soft bed, but not so often as to get the habit. For a placer miner, a wife and children were at best consolation prizes and at worst traps to be avoided. A wife and family usually destined a man to the necessity of working for wages. Sidestepping those kinds of traps could be difficult, but it was at least something a man had some control over. The mining companies threw a much wider and far tighter net. By the beginning of the twentieth century, if you wanted to make a living as a miner you worked for a company. Consequently an attitude developed: "What choice have I got? A man's got to keep body and soul together." But working for wages only took care of the body. The soul is another matter entirely, and for these men it was not being nourished by a church. The food it craved—independence—had been taken away by the mining companies. From most miners' point of view only a "Scissor Bill," a worker who accepts anything and everything the boss visits upon him, could be anything but restive and resentful.[1]

The men who founded the Western Federation of Miners (WFM) in 1893 in Butte, Montana, were figuratively and in some cases literally the sons of placer miners. They embraced the agenda "products for all, profits for none." They had no desire to be a business union, interested exclusively in better pay, safer working conditions, and shorter working hours. Instead, the WFM wanted an end to the wage system entirely. The union echoed the cowboy motto—"Anything's better than wages." In fact, Big Bill Haywood briefly attempted to organize cowboys.[2]

In a discussion of anti-intellectualism among US socialists during the opening decades of the twentieth century, Pulitzer Prize–winning historian Richard Hofstadter accuses western Socialists of adapting "a veritable proletarian mucker pose." He writes:

> The most extreme anti-intellectual position in the party—a veritable proletarian mucker pose—was taken not by the right wingers nor by the self-alienated intellectuals but by Western party members affected by the IWW spirit. The Oregon wing was a good example of this spirit. The story is told that at the party's 1912 convention in Indianapolis the Oregon delegates refused to have dinner in a restaurant that had tablecloths. Thomas Sladden, their state secretary, once removed the cuspidors from the Oregon headquarters because he felt hard boiled, tobacco-chewing proletarians would have no use for such genteel devices.

One wonders how not wanting to eat off tablecloths in a public venue is anti-intellectual. Isn't it more likely the Wobbly-influenced Westerners objected to the tablecloths because they were not accustomed to them in so public and commercial a setting? Their experience of eating with tablecloths would have been on special occasions in an intimate, family setting. To break bread on a tablecloth under the circumstances described by Hofstadter could very well have been viewed by those workingmen as a betrayal of something they held dear. Likewise, Hofstadter's use of the expression "proletarian mucker" demands some interrogation; specifically his choice of the word "mucker," which *Webster's New World Dictionary (Third Edition)* defines as "[slang] a coarse or vulgar person, esp. one without honor; cad." In defense of so severe an epithet one expects more than two anecdotes; the first of which implies that rejecting the use of tablecloths is somehow dishonorable and anti-intellectual, while the second tells us far more about Thomas Sladden's expectations than it does about the attitudes of the workers in question. A sense of how deep class-cultural frictions and prejudices run renders itself visible when a thinker of Richard Hofstadter's caliber rather off-handedly issues so harsh a judgment.

The law assumed violence was standard operating procedure for the Western Federation of Miners. Unsolved murders were habitually considered the union's doing, which made it all the easier for the mining companies to obtain state militia and federal troops when there was "labor unrest." The governors of Idaho, Montana, and Nevada routinely provided militia to employers. The exception is Colorado Governor "Bloody Bridles" Waite, who employed militia to protect strikers from company goons. The other governors used militia to break strikes and fatten campaign contributions. The miners union often had sheriffs and mayors on their side, but those local officials had no control over state militia.

The Western Federation of Miners, which Frank Little joined in 1900, became the soul of the Industrial Workers of the World when that union was founded in 1905. The IWW was assumed to be as violent as the WFM, if not more so. The violence question is particularly germane to a discussion of the western Wobblies as they stand accused of being the most aggressive faction of a union reputed to have a propensity for violence.

Georges Sorel's *Reflections on Violence* is usually said to have provided the newly founded IWW with its "philosophical underpinnings," although journalist J. Anthony Lukas writes that Bill Haywood was "uncomfortable" with radical syndicalism and its French origins. For Sorel, proletarian violence makes "future revolution certain;" said violence "seems to be [the] only means by which the European nations—at present stupefied by humanitarianism—can recover their former energy." According to Sorel, violence will reestablish class divisions, which is the great aim of those "who think of tomorrow and are not hypnotized by the event of the day." The world may be saved, in his view, if the proletariat remains true to revolutionary ideas and "as much as possible" realizes Karl Marx's vision.

Sorel believed he was helping to "ruin the prestige of middle-class culture . . . which up to now has been opposed to the complete development of the 'class war.'" He describes justice as "created to secure the prosperity of production and to permit its free and constantly widening development." He portrays the middle class as devotees to "the principles of the Monarchy and the church." He condemns violence for its own sake: "the acts of savagery performed by the revolutionaries of 1893" were the result of the perpetrators being "*middle-class* revolutionaries" [my emphasis].

The Industrial Workers of the World was severely criticized (and slandered) for its lack of patriotism. Sorel believed syndicalists must deny the idea of patriotism if they are to avoid being corrupted by a middle class bent on alienating workers from revolutionary ideas. This denial of patriotism is not so much a choice but a necessity "imposed by external conditions." Sorel writes: "The essential thing is that for the revolutionary workers anti-patriotism appears [to be] an essential part of Socialism." He is critical of socialists who speak of the flag symbolizing "patriotic, sacred duty" and fiercely opposes a "noisy, garrulous, and lying socialism, which is exploited by ambitious people of every description."

"No God! No Master!"—a slogan employed by militant anti-religious/anti-patriotic Wobblies—offended and oftentimes frightened that portion of the rank and file who had not shed their religious and patriotic sensibilities. Labor historian Philip S. Foner attributes the axiom to a small sect of anarchists. It seems unlikely that a working organizer like Frank Little would publicly support such a statement whatever his private feelings might have been. Raised in a Quaker household, the groundwork for religious belief must certainly have been laid, but there's no evidence of Little practicing a faith apart from the IWW.

On the question of democracy, Sorel believes the greatest danger facing syndicalism was attempting to imitate democracy. Better to remain content, for a time, with "weak and chaotic organizations" rather than be led by syndicates that "would copy the political forms of the middle class." Sorel's central importance to the IWW is found in the following remarks on the gen-

eral strike: "If no myths are accepted by the masses talking of re-
volt indefinitely will never provoke revolutionary action. The
general strike is the myth required." In his view, socialist politicians "so roundly oppose the general strike because they fear losing their power to the workers." A strike was, for Sorel, not just
"a temporary rupture of commercial regulations," but a "phe-
nomenon of war," a step toward replacing rather than reforming
the system.[3]

Philosopher Walter Benjamin's "Critique of Violence" empha-
sizes the importance of Sorel's distinction between the "political
general strike," which the former describes as little more than a
changing of the guard, and the "proletarian general strike," which
is bent on destroying state power. Benjamin goes on to remind us
that so far as "the state, the law" is concerned, the right to strike
does not include the right to commit violence, "but rather to escape from a violence indirectly exercised by the employer." When
strikers commit violence, the legitimacy of the strike is revoked or
criminal charges are filed or, sometimes, both.

On the question of "police violence," Benjamin writes that
police violence is "violence for legal ends . . . but with the simultaneous authority to decide these ends itself within wide limits." He
continues: "The assertion that the ends of police violence are always identical or even connected to those of general law is utterly
untrue. Rather, the 'law' of the police really marks the point at
which the state, whether from impotence or because of the imma-
nent connections within any legal system, *can no longer guarantee
through the legal system empirical ends that it desires at any price to at-
tain* [my emphasis]. Therefore, the police intervene for 'security

reasons' in countless cases where no clear legal situation exists . . . [thereby] accompanying the citizen as a brutal encumbrance through a life regulated by ordinances, or simply supervising him." Benjamin is of course describing police violence as an instrument of social control.

Perhaps we discover the key to the IWW's use of what is routinely described as violence by considering the relationship of violence to action. Toward this end, political theorist Hannah Arendt offers some useful ideas when she writes: "All the properties of creativity ascribed to life in manifestations of violence and power actually belong to the faculty of action, and I think it can be shown that no other human activity has suffered to such an extent by the Progress of the modern age." Arendt recognizes that violence, like power, is a form of action; and action has been severely hampered by "the Progress of the modern age." If violence and power are manifestations of action, and modern Progress impedes action, what else might we say about modern Progress? Is it dependent on the administration of justice as defined above by Georges Sorel? In *The Illusions of Progress* Sorel describes progress as "the adornment of the mind that, free of prejudice, sure of itself, and trusting in the future, has created a philosophy *assuring the happiness of all those who possess the means of living well*" [my emphasis]. For such a progress to endure must action on the part of those who do not "possess the means of living well" be suppressed?[4]

Frank Little's devotion to direct action is beyond question. Like his western fellow workers, Little was essentially a collectivist and an anti-centralist. On the question of action, Arendt observes: "[It] is the function of all action, as distinguished from mere behavior, to interrupt what otherwise would have proceeded automatically and therefore predictably." By attempting to act rather than just behave, the Wobblies clashed headlong with an automatic, predictable, business-as-usual credo that World War One did a great deal to solidify.[5]

The IWW adopted the WFM policy of taking in any worker who could produce a valid union card regardless of race, color, or creed. The union went a step further by organizing migratory workers, particularly the wheat harvesters of the great plain states, who had been pointedly ignored by the other unions. These workers moved from job to job by hopping freight trains and living in what they themselves described as "hobo jungles." In November 1914, *Solidarity*, the IWW newspaper, described them as "nomadic workers of the West. They embody the very spirit of the IWW. Half industrial worker, half vagabond adventurer. They may become the guerrillas of the revolution." This statement, made the year war began in Europe, stepped into dangerous territory. There was no place for a workers' revolution in what would become a mythologized American West of cowboys and Indians. Revolution conjured up images too topical and frightening for the American middle class and its politicians. Nigel Anthony Sellars in *Oil, Wheat, and Wobblies* seriously questions IWW assumptions about the western migratory worker's radical inclinations. He believes the union too easily accepted "the erroneous idea that migratory workers were the vanguard of the revolution." One could readily place Frank Little among those who made such an error—if indeed it was an error.

By examining more closely the environment in which he lived and worked, and by discussing the IWW out west in relation to the

IWW back east, we can gain a deeper understanding of Frank Little, the man often described as "Half-Indian, Half-white man, and all Wobbly."[6]

Writing in 1915, University of Washington economist Carleton H. Parker said that western Wobblies were recruited from among the homeless, men with "no sex life except the abnormal . . . hunted and scorned by society; normal leadership, emulation, constructiveness is unknown to them." Reading the above one would think the professor was a psychologist rather than an economist.[7] Parker's description does, however, offer an explanation of why the other unions believed these particular workers could not be organized. But by 1914–15, "emulation" and "constructiveness" were not "unknown" to a sizable number of these workers as by then they had emulated Frank Little and other free-speech fighters by participating in several free speech actions. (Fighting for the First Amendment of the US Constitution seems constructive to me.) If by "normal leadership" Parker means a leadership issuing orders from on high and treating those to whom said orders are issued as subordinate and inferior, then his use of the term is accurate. Of course a collectivist western IWW did not care to have any such "normal leadership."

Despite the remarks mentioned above, Parker was far more sympathetic to the western migratory worker than most of his peers. In the titular essay of *The Casual Laborer and Other Essays*, Parker refers to 1913–1914 as "the period of the migratory worker." He points out that by 1910 there were ten million four hundred thousand unskilled male workers in the United States. Three and a half million of them "moved, by discharge or quitting, so regularly from one work town to another that they could be called migratory labor." Among the unskilled "one-fourth of the adult fathers of families" earned under $400 annually while half earned less than $600 a year. At the time, $800 a year was needed if a family was to live decently. Parker writes: "Unemployment, destitution, uncared-for-sickness was a monotonous familiarity to them." Workers without children to support often earned a "jungle stake" then quit. The stake (usually $15) was enough to live in a hobo jungle for months. Parker tells us western Wobblies routinely severed all connection with blood kin. Might they have thought such a rupture necessary if they were to truly shed capitalist America's influence on them, or might their rootless, kinless way of life been the closest thing to freedom they believed available to them? Whatever the reasons behind their alienation, Frank Little often lived among and became known to many of them as the hobo agitator.

According to a study Parker conducted for California Governor Hiram W. Johnson, 67 percent of the hoboes were "floating" and did not want steady work. He found that 76 percent were unmarried, although a Chicago study put that figure at 90 percent. Seventy-seven percent were alcoholics, and 26 percent admitted to having jail records. He goes on to say an unnamed "California state official believes data shows a widespread practice of homosexual acts" in the overcrowded, heatless hobo jungles. Parker believed the western Wobblies consisted entirely of migratory workers, who were thought of at the time as hobo-laborers: "a hobo miner, hobo lumberjack, the blanket stiff [farm laborer]." He wrote: "the American [western] IWW is a neglected and lonely hobo worker, usually undernourished and in need of medical care." Again he analyzes

Wobblies from a psycho-social perspective, and his only comment on the IWW's goal of abolishing the wage system and introducing industrial democracy is to call it "bizarre."

Historian Robert L. Tyler's assessment of the western Wobbly parallels Carlton Parker's but without the pathology. Tyler speaks of the IWW as "a small fraternity of itinerant rebels and hoboes" who turned to the union "because it supplied a home and a meaning for their aimless lives." He continues: "Structurally, the I.W.W. appealed to them because it made no political demands upon them, because it charged low initial fees and dues, because it allowed seasonal workers to transfer from one constituent union to another without red tape or new fees. It appealed psychologically because it satisfied social needs and because it seemed to be an organization really their own, not something created for them by middle-class socialists, welfare workers, or the Salvation Army." Historian Arnon Gutfeld believes Tyler's portrait of the western Wobbly is far more dependent on myth than fact, but however we classify the latter's comments they offer us insights well worth our consideration. Tyler writes: "Zealous, individualistic, and free from ordinary social constraints, Wobblies acted with humor or fanaticism, from idealistic motives or from malice, but always with a raggedy dash, they were activists, not theorists. . . . They acted primarily out of their itch to bring the battle to the 'master class,' and made hardly any effort to spell out their program in subtle detail."[8]

In his essay, "The I.W.W. and the West," Tyler argues that the Wobbly of "legend" is a westerner by "character and habitat, thus making it another symbol within the complex myth of the West, that migrating American region of primitive vitality that serves as heroic age and seedbed of our national *virtu* and *pietas*." But, he concludes, the facts do not often square with the legend. Tyler believes the western Wobblies "serve as mythic symbols, as spiky individualists setting off the dreary conformism and money-grubbing of a decaying American capitalism." But the fact is, as he writes, the IWW's first big successes as a labor union occurred in the East; first in 1909 in McKee's Rocks, Pennsylvania, during the Pressed Steel Car Strike, and then during the 1912 Lawrence Textile Workers Strike in Massachusetts. Later in this chapter, Lawrence is discussed as a 'western-style' strike. Tyler would very probably question the terms of said discussion as he argues that tactics "presumed to be so typically 'Western' in the minds of regional authors had their exact counterparts in as un-Western a place as New York City. 'Free-speech fights' and similar guerrilla tactics were not in fact limited to the West." But the success of the free-speech struggles in Missoula, Spokane, and Fresno, California, offers some evidence for the tactics employed in those struggles being, in large part, imported by eastern Wobblies.

In another essay of Carlton Parker's, entitled "IWW," written during the intense government repression of the IWW, which shortly followed Frank Little's death, Parker no doubt meant to help the Wobblies, a few of whom he knew personally, when he wrote that they were the "psychological by-product of the neglected childhood of industrial America. It is discouraging to see the problem today almost exclusively examined regarding its relation to patriotism and conventional commercial mortality." The paternalism of his remarks leaps to the eye and has deep historical roots. In his magnificent *The Making of the English Working Classes* E. P. Thompson writes of the need for industrial stability, a stable work force, and body of experienced workers making the creation of new managerial methods mandatory; so new forms of paternalism were practiced in 1830s English cotton mills. Approximately eighty years later, in a letter to Theodore Roosevelt, US Steel director Frank Munsey spoke of "paternal guardianship of the people" because they needed "the sustaining and guiding hand of the state." Munsey believed the state's work is "to think for the people and plan for the people."[9]

Where Parker is paternalistic and Tyler plain spoken and to a certain degree sympathetic, historian Christopher Lasch is empathetic as he writes: "In the American West, the ideal of independence was associated not with the small proprietor's control over his household, his land or shop, and his tools but with the wandering life of the unattached male. It was not surprising that the Wobblies of the West glorified the hobo, the drifter, the 'nomadic worker of the West,' in the words of its newspaper, *Solidarity*." The West was still a "man's country" that drew adventurers from Germany, England, and France. Lasch continues: "Those who admired the Wobblies from a distance likewise emphasized its Western origins." But by the twentieth century the independence to be found out West was no longer easily attained, if possible at all. Nigel Sellars cites "an editor of the IWW's *Industrial Union Bulletin* noting in 1909, 'But unlike the pioneer seeking a homestead and finding it, the modern wage-worker who 'goes west' has no alternative except to hunt for a master.'"

Historian and cultural critic Lincoln Steffens referred to the 1912 Lawrence Strike as a "western strike in the east," saying it had a western "spirit" and employed "methods" new to the East. The conflict was set in motion when on the first day of 1912 a new Massachusetts state law took effect, cutting the hours women and minor children were allowed to work from fifty-six to fifty-four per week. On its first payday of the new year the American Woolen Company complied with the law but also enacted a pro rata wage reduction of its own. The mid-January strike of approximately ten thousand workers included four mills. Immigrant women with families to support were being paid eight dollars and seventy-six cents a week. When those wages were reduced without notice, Polish weavers shut down their mill and the other three mills shortly followed. The IWW swung into action and kept striking workers too busy to allow them to begin brooding. Mass meetings were held, parades organized, and soup kitchens set up. Food and fuel had to be obtained for fifty thousand people, 60 percent of Lawrence's entire population. The city's mayor called in the state militia to suppress a parade and a striker named Anna Lopizzo was shot dead. Witnesses identified a policeman as the shooter, but Wobbly organizers Joseph Ettor and Arturo Giovannitti, neither of whom was on the scene, were charged with the murder. The state claimed the two men arranged the killing with an unknown assailant.

In February, seven to ten thousand strikers moving in one long picket line marched through the mill districts wearing "Don't be a scab" armbands. As the strike progressed and food became increasingly scarce, the union employed a tactic occasionally used in Europe but new to the United States. Children ages four to fourteen were sent to fellow workers and sympathizers in other cities; two hundred went to New York and another thirty-five to Barre,

Vermont. Citing a city ordinance about child neglect, authorities forbade any more strikers' children from leaving Lawrence. When forty children, proceeding in an orderly fashion with their parents nearby, tried to board a train bound for Philadelphia, police on horseback attacked, wielding clubs and putting youngsters in danger of being trampled. Several people were hospitalized and, according to historian Howard Zinn, a pregnant woman lost her baby as a result of being beaten. Meanwhile, the IWW was accused of plotting a series of bombings until further investigation showed the culprit to be an undertaker with connections to American Woolen Company. Finally, the strikers won a 5 percent raise for the highest paid workers, an 11 percent increase for the lowest paid, and a promise that no reprisals would be taken against any strikers. The strike, led by Big Bill Haywood and Elizabeth Gurley Flynn, earned a good deal of sympathy for the IWW, and Joseph Ettor and Arturo Giovannitti were acquitted.

In the first volume of John Dos Passos's USA: *The 42nd Parallel*, we find Mac, a western Wobbly. Dos Passos's portrait of Mac is no doubt romanticized, yet he manages to give his readers a sense of the circumstances and complexities shaping the lives of men like Mac while Carleton Parker's statistics and psychology pin living beings to a display board like so many butterflies. The light Parker sheds, useful as it may be (who can deny the potential utility of statistics and theory?) is too often devoid of the blood coursing presence of life being lived.

Having grown tired of being on the bum, Mac and his buddy Ike sign up for a lumber camp up the Snake River in Oregon. On the train ride to the camp, among Swedes and Finns, they are the

only English speakers. Once they arrive the food is "so rotten . . .
the bunkhouse so filthy . . . the foreman so hard-boiled . . . they lit
out at the end of a couple of days, on the bum again." Mac and
Ike were two of the "floaters" Parker writes about. The pair part
ways along the road, and Mac eventually drifts to San Francisco
where he meets Maisie Spencer, who works in an Emporium. They
fall in love and consummate their relationship. Mac has printing
skills and the newly formed IWW sends him to help editor Fred
Hoff of the sympathetic *The Nevada Workman* in Goldfield, Nevada, during the strike of 1905; in which Frank Little participated
as a WFM affiliate. Arriving at his destination, Mac is confronted
with a charged atmosphere. State militia are keeping a vigilant
watch and Mac must pass himself off as a seller of schoolbooks
and the like in order to be allowed into town. Amidst violence and
political tension, Mac learns that Maisie is pregnant and carries
the letter announcing that fact in his pocket. He begins to feel
"uncomfortable" at a hall filled with "the odor of plug tobacco . . .
the shanty smell of oil lamps and charred firewood and greasy fry-
ing pans and raw whiskey." The constant clearing of throats and
movements of men waiting for the meeting to begin make him
"uneasy." When Mac tells Fred Hoff he is going to return to San
Francisco and marry Maisie, the editor says Mac's "first duty's to
the workin' class." Mac replies that he is not abandoning the struggle but needs to make more money now that a child is on the way.
Hoff replies, "A wobbly ought not to have any wife and children,
not till after the revolution."

Mac asks another of his fellow workers, a man named Ben
Evans, what he should do about Maisie and is told if she was worth

marrying she would not have had sex with him in the first place. Mac says he doesn't "see it like that." Evans replies that he does not trust any woman. His final word on the matter is short and not so sweet; the long-standing ethos of rambling men—"love 'em and leave 'em." Mac turns to alcohol and travels to Ludlow, Colorado. "After those bleak dusty months in Goldfield he needed a woman." After witnessing the drowning of a pregnant girl, and fearing "Maisie might kill herself," Mac continues on to San Francisco where he and Maisie are married without saying anything to her folks.

In the conservative fiction being read by the great mass of Americans back east, the western Wobblies were a violent group of fanatics, an image the immensely popular Zane Grey made considerable use of in *Desert of Wheat*, in which Wobblies torch machinery with abandon. The image is not entirely false. Torching the machinery of exploitative employers was, at times, a necessary weapon. We need to ask ourselves what other choice did the Wobblies, like the Luddites before them, have? They certainly could not expect help or protection from the authorities, for the western Wobblies were considered the worst of a bad bunch. According to a capitalist mythology that "honored" hard-working factory workers while leaving them in the breach, the eastern IWW rank and file were making America a first-rate industrial power. They endured the prison-like atmosphere of their workplace, the long hours, poor ventilation, horrible living conditions, and low pay. While they did not do so with the quiet desperation the middle and upper classes preferred, they did stick it out. The western IWW, on the other hand, was at least in part a refuge for those who fled the factory-worker life and the uniformity it required. Consequently they were habitually portrayed as lazy, and IWW was often said to stand for "I Won't Work." The question of uniformity's depleting, even deadening, impact on human beings is ignored.

Writing during the opening years of the twentieth century, sociologist Max Weber speaks eloquently of capitalism's need for uniformity: "That powerful tendency towards uniformity in life which today so immensely aids the capitalistic interest in the standardization of production, had its ideal foundation in the repudiation of the idolatry of the flesh." With the coming of the factory, human flesh became machine as never before. As E. P. Thompson points out, "machines symbolized the encroachment of the factory system" on the individual. A conflict arose from a central fact that fleshless machines were each constructed for a specific range of actions, while the fleshed machines, also known as human beings, incarnated a potentially limitless range of actions and, thus, demanded a conditioning their fleshless counterparts did not. For this task religion and language were interwoven as Weber explains: "It does not yet hold, with Franklin, that time is money, but the proposition is true in a certain spiritual sense. It [time] is infinitely valuable because every hour lost is lost to labour for the glory of God. Thus inactive contemplation is also valueless or even directly reprehensible if it is at the expense of one's daily work. For it is less pleasing to God than the active performance of his will in a calling." President Calvin Coolidge described the connection between religion and factory more pointedly, if simplistically, when he said: "The man who builds a factory builds a temple. The man who works there worships there." In the name of said temple and its products-for-profit, inactive contemplation was transformed into a vice. One's inner life, the stuff upon which individualism is nourished, became suspect in so far as it might interfere with the factory worker's efficiency. Let us also not forget: Workers spent the great bulk of their waking hours in the factory. Therefore, should it not be expected that at least some of those who clung most fiercely to their inner lives, their individual selves, "lit out for the Territory?"[10]

Those men are analogous to runaway slaves, the eastern factories being their plantations. As historian M. I. Finley points out, since ancient times "fierce penalties" have been levied against anyone who aided runaway slaves. The western IWW came to the aid of runaways from the factory system. Historian Joseph R. Conlin refers to the western IWW as a "social organization, a workingmen's fraternal lodge." The union hall served as library/reading room, meeting place, and dance hall. It was a "surrogate church," the center of workers' social life in "dismal and isolated industrial towns." Nigel Sellars takes up Conlin's surrogate church idea when he addresses the IWW's commitment "to build a new society within the shell of the old" by working to create "an alternative workers' subculture . . . to overcome religious and ethnic differences among the workers and to compensate for a lack of stable social institutions." In Frank Little's home state and elsewhere, IWW job delegates served as "evangelists for the struggle against the new corporate order." Despite these spiritual-communal considerations, a number of organizers, particularly those from the union's eastern wing, felt that western Wobblies needed to stop worshipping, as Conlin points out, "the Great God 'individual freedom.'" On this issue I suspect Frank Little was ambivalent. He was almost certainly happy as a freelance IWW organizer and agitator, out of the mines and enjoying his largely nomadic life. I suspect he kept his ear to the ground and followed his instincts. His election to the General Executive Board would certainly have put much tighter reins on his freedom. At the same time, Little's allegiance to the IWW and worker solidarity makes it entirely possible he came to seriously question the freedom he cherished, knowing it might well impede the union's aims and potential for growth.

Some of his fellow Wobblies may have thought of Frank Little as a showboat who comes into town, creates a big stir, then moves on, leaving the local workers only temporarily better off. Among the largely Marxist eastern IWW organizers, Little's direct action was probably conceived as anarchistic, albeit nonviolent, propaganda by the deed; a useful first step that often gained public sympathy and invariably attracted potential members, but fell short of building a strong and sustainable labor union. His eastern counterparts may have thought of Little as, at heart, an adventurer and feared those he attracted to the union might likewise be mere adventurers.

A comparison of eastern and western Wobbly policies and points of view offers further insight into the challenges Little and his western comrades faced as they fought to maintain themselves as individuals while at the same time remaining faithful to the worker solidarity so highly valued by the Industrial Workers of the World. In the East the IWW felt that the partially assimilated European immigrant workers, who composed the bulk of the union's rank and file, needed a firm centralized direction, a clear and strong, traditional organizational structure. The eastern

IWW had no intention of taking the kinds of chances about which Georges Sorel wrote. The collectivist practices of the fully assimilated western Wobblies, who were far more likely to have been born in the United States, were tolerated by the eastern IWW—at least until 1915. By that time, Bill Haywood and the majority of the five-person General Executive Board (GEB), upon which Frank Little now sat, were demanding more control by headquarters in curbing what they called "fruitless free-speech fights and propaganda battles." These free-speech fights were fought in order to secure the IWW's right to bring its message directly to the workers in the street, as several cities had passed ordinances preventing the union from doing so. Joseph R. Conlin thinks the IWW abandoned free-speech fights partly because the union's "revolutionary conscience" realized it had better things to do. He seems to overlook the pressure exerted by the war in Europe against free speech and that pressure's impact on revolutionary activity of any kind. Mightn't a "*revolutionary* [my emphasis] conscience" more profoundly show itself by struggling for free speech rather than abandoning the issue?

The eastern IWW had long complained about the huge turnover in the West's membership, attributing that turnover to a lack of central control. In 1913, western and southern IWW locals "sought a decentralization of power on the grounds that every city and town was the center of some particular agricultural or commercial activity." Robert Tyler claims "anarchical Decentralizers" wished to abolish the union's Chicago headquarters as well as "all central authority in the IWW. That same year, the General Executive Board criticized those same "anarchical Decentralizers," largely the western hobo Wobblies, for being talkers and dreamers who could not be enticed onto "a picket line to fight the boss."

The East favored centralization for reasons already cited. It was assumed the GEB knew more about existing conditions than the locals and could, therefore, keep an eye out for local hotheads who might involve the union in a "futile and injurious battle." The paternalism here is stark. We can see why such a policy would have wounded, if not angered, many of the western rank and file. Professor Conlin characterizes the IWW as espousing "a participatory sort of democracy, in which, although the authority was centralized, all members shared in that authority." The eastern IWW's superior numbers and its commitment to a "strong" and "traditional" form of centralization make it difficult to believe an equitable sharing of authority existed between eastern and western Wobblies.

Perhaps the westerners were simply victims of the rule of numbers inherent in democracy and the decline of human action in the modern age. Kevin Phillips's observation, in his fascinating study *Wealth and Democracy*, is pertinent: "In the nineteenth century Thomas Carlyle could describe history as the sum of innumerable biographies. In the twentieth century, economic history, at least, began to exchange statistical drama—the gyrations of median income, the quiet revolutions in income tax, the proliferations of telecommunications, the dimensions of speculative bubbles, the whiplashing of markets, the computerization of the world—for stalwart personalities. The First World War was an early transition point." If Nigel Sellars is correct, and by the first decade of the twentieth century the "Wild West" no longer stood outside and apart from an industrial order dedicated to an ever-increasing mechanization and standardization, the demise of the western Wobbly with or without a world war was inevitable.

Individualism and factionalism did not prevent the IWW, east and west alike, from standing firmly together on two basic points. First, most of the union's members did not have the right to vote: in the East because they were recent immigrants, not yet citizens; in the West, they were too nomadic and had no stable address. Second, the vision of One Big Union for all wageworkers provided the foundation upon which the IWW stood in its most monolithic form. The vision (Sorel's myth) went like this: a single union of all workers would bring about a general strike, which would, in turn, bring the economy to its knees, thereby forcing factory owners to turn over the running of industry to the workers. Consequently, industrial democracy would ensue as the capitalistic government collapsed. It was an inspiring vision, but no match for the blood and the glory of 'the war to end all wars.'

Yet, this small union (by IWW leader Vincent St. John's count, there were twenty-five thousand; by Carleton Parker's, it was seventy-five thousand) had managed for a period of eight years (1909–1917) to have a tremendous impact on the masses of American workers, as evidenced by a Congressional Commission on Industrial Relations report that, even though IWW membership was small, "as 'a spirit and a vocabulary' [the IWW] permeates to a large extent enormous masses of workers, particularly among the unskilled and migratory laborers." Frank Little did a substantial portion of his work among those workers, and in some ways might be said to fit Carleton Parker's description of the western hobo Wobbly. But probably long before 1909 when his leadership in the Missoula free-speech fight came to the notice of IWW headquarters in Chicago, Little along with with other organizers, many of whom have been lost to history, took on the often thankless job of transforming hobo jungles into communities. In order to accomplish their task, Little and his comrades first drove out the predators (card sharks, thieves, con men), banned the use of alcohol, instituted proper toilet facilities, rode herd on the drug addicts, and generally established order. Perhaps most importantly they brought men society had turned its back on into the free-speech fights, which, whatever else they may or may not have been, sought to preserve a fundamental principle upon which this nation was built.

Frank Little's motives were probably not entirely altruistic; but then human motives very rarely are. He had begun working as a miner when he was nineteen years old. His participation in free-speech fights brought him out of the pits and into fresh air. Those same struggles gave him an opportunity to escape the back-breaking, spirit-numbing toil that all too easily smothered a miner's humanity. It gave him an opportunity to help create a world in which he would no longer be under another man's thumb. As an individual, Frank Little frequently appears to be seeking a system of his own so as not to be a slave in another man's. As an agitator/organizer he showed his mettle by helping others show theirs rather than drown in a sea of "lonely, undernourished" men.

# CHAPTER TWO
# **Free-Speech Fights**

From 1909 until 1914, when the union virtually abandoned such fights, Frank Little played a prominent role in the free-speech struggles engaged in by the Industrial Workers of the World. On at least two occasions he recruited free-speech "soldiers" from hobo jungles then either sent or accompanied them by freight train more than a thousand miles away to take part in an action. Though the union had been involved in free-speech struggles for four years, an official position on such engagements did not appear until the September 4, 1913, issue of the *Industrial Worker:* "We have little desire to enter into these scraps, [but] neither will we stand by and see our only hope taken from us—the right to educate the working class."

Like Thomas Paine and Michael Bakunin, the IWW viewed ignorance as an essential collaborator in the continued smooth functioning of governments. In his *Rights of Man*, Paine proclaims: "Reason and Ignorance, the opposites of each other, influence the great bulk of Mankind. If either of these can be rendered sufficiently extensive in a country, the machinery of government goes easily on. Reason obeys itself; and *Ignorance submits to whatever is dictated to it*" [my emphasis]. In *God and the State*, Bakunin says of ignorance and government: "The people, unfortunately, are still very ignorant, are kept in ignorance by the systematic efforts of all governments, who consider this ignorance, not without good reason, as one of the essential conditions of their power."

The IWW free-speech actions might fittingly be described as direct-action seminars in how to understand and combat those forces that on a daily, bread-and-butter basis exploited migratory laborers. Yet, it is not until Little's crusade against America's entry into World War One, his last free-speech fight, do we encounter the full implications of Paine's and Bakunin's comments on government utilization of ignorance to achieve its own ends.

IWW free-speech actions have oftentimes been viewed as romantic idealism rather than genuine labor organizing. This assessment seems to ignore a basic fact: most of the free-speech actions occurred when city ordinances were passed prohibiting IWW speakers from holding street meetings to educate and organize workers who were being cheated by fraudulent employment agencies that sent workers to jobs from which they were fired shortly after receiving their first paychecks. The agencies took the largest part of those checks as finder's fees then split the fees with the employer. The IWW was clearly acting in these cases as a labor union coming to the aid of exploited workers and, in so doing, taking a first step toward organizing those workers. The hobo workers who participated in many of the free-speech actions undoubtedly harbored a certain amount of resentment towards a society which generally thought of them as scum, but that does not mean that resentment entirely controlled their actions. As a labor organizing policy, the free-speech struggles were not quantitatively successful, but the quality of the spirit generated by the free-speech fighters played a central role in the Wobblies's huge impact on the labor movement.

This chapter focuses on eight free-speech actions. Various sources put Frank Little on the scene at five of those eight actions. The evidence in question is usually grounded in newspaper reports of Little being arrested and statements by other participants. I have included three other actions because there are substantial reasons for believing he took part in them, despite the lack of documented evidence.

## MISSOULA

In 1909, Frank Little and four or five other Wobblies were already on the scene in Missoula, Montana, when Vincent St. John, at the IWW headquarters in Chicago, sent Elizabeth Gurley Flynn and her husband, Jack Jones, to recruit timber workers and establish an IWW union hall. While Philip S. Foner seems ready to assume no real organizing took place before Flynn and Jones arrived, we should not forget that Little first served as an organizer in 1903 when, as a member of the Western Federation of Miners, he worked in the Clifton Morenci Metcalf area copper camps. By

1909 he was a seasoned veteran and would hardly have required the presence of Flynn and Jones to begin organizing.

On September 28, 1909, Little was arrested for reading the Declaration of Independence out loud on a street corner. The Declaration would become his document of choice in future free-speech fights. While we can only speculate as to why he chose that particular document, it may well have fulfilled a three-fold purpose. One, along with the Bill of Rights, the Declaration of Independence is the most American of documents as it announces the humanist underpinnings of a new and, at least potentially, egalitarian nation. Little was fond of referring to himself as a "real American." Writing about Little in her autobiography, Elizabeth Gurley Flynn writes: "He was part Indian and spoke of himself as 'a real American.' 'The rest of you are immigrants,' he said." Two, the Declaration is a glaring example of a garden-variety hypocrisy Frank Little was sure to have detested. Its statement "all men are equal with certain inalienable rights" did not apply, within the workings of the American system, to Native Americans or black people (regardless of their gender) or white females or white males who were not property owners. Little may have viewed the act of reading the Declaration in the street as a particularly sharp slap in the face to the system of exclusion, and to the citizens who supported the law he was breaking. Three, Little's reading of the document could help make public the Declaration's revolutionary components, such as the sentence, "When in the course of human events, it becomes necessary for one people to dissolve the political bonds which have connected them with another," or the pronouncement, "but when a long train of usurpations, pursuing invariably the same Object evinces a design to reduce them under absolute Despotism, it is right, it is their [people's] duty, to throw off such Government, and to provide new Guards for their future security."

Little and the other Wobblies originally on the scene were arrested for defying the ordinance against street speaking, and they were sentenced to fifteen days in jail. Two days later, a call went out in the *Industrial Worker*, requesting a show of support for the free-speech fighters in Missoula, and boxcars of Wobblies were soon on their way to Montana. Within a few days, the city jail was overflowing, so the authorities turned a fire station into a second jail. Wobbly prisoners loudly protested their captivity in speech and song, day and night, until their neighbors from across the street, patrons of the town's main hotel, bitterly complained about the noise.

Little was arrested more than once for street speaking, as were a number of others. With the jails jam-packed and the cost of feeding these prisoners steadily rising, authorities began releasing first offenders as quickly as possible. But when the offense was repeated, the authorities had no choice but to arrest the lawbreakers again. IWW street meetings were often scheduled so as to put arrested speakers in jail in time for supper. The authorities reacted by attempting to release prisoners before breakfast, but the men refused to leave their cells. They demanded jury trials; having been arrested they expected their full constitutional rights. At a public forum held in a theater upstairs from the IWW union hall, US senator Robert B. Lafollette defended the embattled Wobblies. The ordinance banning street speakers was repealed shortly thereafter.

## SPOKANE

During the early years of the twentieth century, Spokane, Washington, served as a magnet for migratory workers from logging camps, saw mills, construction camps, and commercial farms. These drastically underpaid seasonal laborers, whose living conditions during their working months were routinely overcrowded and unsanitary, regularly wintered in Spokane. Their work season kept them on the move, so IWW organizers had to catch them in the winter.

The Spokane free-speech struggle surfaced in the winter of 1909–1910, but the groundwork began in late 1908 when the IWW initiated its DON'T BUY JOBS! Campaign. The union had documented hundreds of cases of workers bilked of their wages. As in Missoula, employment agencies were scamming desperate workers, sometimes sending them to non-existent jobs, but more often employing the same tactic as their Missoula counterparts. The scam worked like this: an agency sent a worker to a job where he worked for a week, sometimes two, but when the time came for him to be paid, a fee was extracted, which took virtually all the worker's wages. The agency and the employer split the fee and the worker's employment was terminated. It became known among IWW organizers as "perpetual motion"—one workman leaving the job, another working it, and a third on his way to it. Joe Hill wrote a song titled "Mr. Block," about this particular brand of larceny.[1] The struggle began and a call went out for Wobbly reinforcements.

Spokane's mayor responded to an invasion of boxcar-riding Wobblies by offering a compromise. He would release those Wobblies already in jail if the IWW agreed to abide by a higher court decision on one of the ordinances prohibiting street speaking. The union refused. The police asked the IWW to hold its meetings in a public park rather than the street, and the union again refused.

The Spokane employment agencies were better organized than they had been in Missoula. The Associated Agencies of Spokane complained about traffic congestion and urged the city council to ban public meetings "on the street, sidewalk, or alleys." The council complied. The ordinance covered its bases so specifically because Wobblies had moved their meetings from the street to the sidewalk and finally into the alleys. As he had in Missoula, Frank Little defied the ordinance by reading the Declaration of Independence aloud in public and was arrested and jailed. Once again the IWW press issued a call for support, and boxcars full of Wobbly-hoboes invaded Spokane. When the city jail overflowed, prisoners were transferred to the unheated Franklin School building and fed one-third of a baker's loaf of bread and a tin cup of water per day. Elizabeth Gurley Flynn took part in the action and was jailed. Her description of Frank Little provides a clue to his reputation as a dangerous man: "He was tall and dark, with black hair and black eyes, a slender, gentle and soft-spoken man. His one eye gave him a misleading sinister appearance."

The struggle escalated and the authorities resorted to torture. Three prisoners died of those abuses, and Little was savagely beaten more than once, as were several other Wobblies. A news wire service heard about what was going on and the city became known as "Barbarous Spokane." The IWW sued a city official named Burns who panicked and blamed local fat cats for ordering the beatings. On March 5, 1910, the city council revoked the ordinance against street meetings, which had not ever been enforced against the Salvation Army, and swore to leave IWW offices alone as long as the union dropped its damage suit. The struggle came to a close, an apparent IWW victory, but the city council's promise was not kept for long. This kind of short-lived victory prompted Robert L. Tyler to remark: "Thus the I.W.W. won an intoxicating victory at the cost of much suffering and three deaths from starvation, chilling, and the brutality of guards, a victory in a somewhat unnecessary struggle that neither built up its union nor appreciably hastened the revolution." Tyler offers no explanation for his dismissal of the Spokane action as "a somewhat unnecessary struggle" thereby ignoring the importance of educating and defending the rights of exploited workers. One seriously wonders what was "necessary" in his scheme of things.

Despite the union's nonviolent activities, there were those on the left who feared the IWW would resort to bomb throwing in Spokane. In a letter to Olive M. Johnson, Daniel DeLeon expressed his fears: "I have all along been apprehensive that some of those knipperdollings [Wobblies] would throw a bomb." A former Yale professor whose politics had cost him his job, DeLeon, along with Vincent St. John and William Trautmann, took control of the 1906 IWW convention. Two years later, DeLeon parted ways with St. John when the latter embraced those western workers the former described as the "bummery" and the "overall brigade." DeLeon was pleased to see at least "some of the Spokane capitalists [knew] there are socialists who spurn I-am-a-bummism, and all that thereby hangs." Little, the hobo agitator, would surely have been part of the "bummery" Daniel DeLeon rejected.

## FRESNO

The trouble in Fresno, California, began when a contractor paying what Philip S. Foner calls "starvation wages" could not find workers and complained to the police, saying the IWW had purposely created a labor shortage. The charge was true enough, but conveniently overlooked the unsatisfactory wages which made the laborers so susceptible to the union's message. Police began breaking up IWW street meetings. On August 20, 1910, Frank Little was arrested as he stood on the street preparing to speak. Over the next few weeks he was arrested several more times—once for reading the Declaration of Independence; other times for addressing workers on street corners—and was jailed and released. Little had come to Fresno to found IWW Local 66, organizing agricultural and construction workers, and to see his brother W. F. Little, who at the time was also a Wobbly.[2]

A week after his arrest in August, Frank Little was quoted in *Solidarity* saying, "If we had the streets so we could get to the workers, we could be building a good fighting organization." He also warned of trouble brewing in Fresno. The local press had taken a savage stand against "outside agitators." A *Fresno Herald* editorial, reprinted in the *Industrial Worker*, wrote, "For men to come here with the express purpose of creating trouble, a whipping post and a cat-o-nine-tails well seasoned by being soaked in salt water is none too harsh a treatment for peace-breakers." (The price of said peace for those being exploited is, of course, not considered.) Little wired IWW headquarters saying: "F. H. Little sentenced by perjured jury to 25 days in jail. A police conspiracy to get organizer Little out of town."

Little created an explosion of sorts when he told Fresno police officers they were being exploited and advised them to go on strike. The officers' contract stated that they were to work eight-hour shifts, but ten-hour workdays were the norm. When Police Chief Shaw heard about the hobo agitator's advice, he was outraged. The December 17 issue of *Solidarity* quotes him as saying: "The idea of telling the police they ought to go on strike!" He reacted officially by immediately revoking the IWW's permit to speak on the street. The action seriously hindered the growth of Local 66. Even though Little came to trial and was acquitted, his advice to the police may well have been seen by eastern Wobbly organizers, and perhaps some westerners too, as unnecessarily provoking authorities to the detriment of the union.

During his time in jail, Little was one of ninety-four prisoners housed in a forty-seven foot by twenty-eight foot bullpen. By California state standards, there was sufficient air for only five men. He organized a hunger strike. The prisoners threatened to starve themselves to death, leaving the expense of their funerals and the ensuing bad publicity on the county. Little was moved to a single cell and spent twenty-eight days in solitary confinement. Having no desire to see any wire service stories referring to Fresno as "barbarous," the city gave in to the prisoners' demands.

## SAN DIEGO

Emma Goldman and Ben Reitman's trip to San Diego on May 15, 1912, brought some long-standing emotions and issues to a head and set in motion a flood of violence. Six months earlier, in December 1911, a grand jury had recommended "Soapbox Row" be cleared and street speaking prohibited. How long the speaking that produced "Soapbox Row" had been going on is uncertain, but it is safe to assume the numbers of those listening were on the increase; otherwise, why prohibit the speakers?

Joyce L. Kornbluh's instructive anthology *Rebel Voices* cites the following "unsigned verses," which originally appeared in the *Industrial Worker* of May 1, 1912. The song served as a battle cry for the San Diego free-speech fight.

### WE'RE BOUND FOR SAN DIEGO
(Tune: "The Wearing of the Green")

In that town called San Diego when the workers
try to talk
The cops will smash them with a say and tell 'em
"take a walk."
They throw them in a bull pen, and they feed
them rotten beans,
And they call that "law and order in that city, so
it seems."
*Chorus*
We're bound for San Diego, you better join us

now.

If they don't quit, you bet there'll be an
awful row.

We're coming by the hundreds, will be joined by
hundreds more.

So join at once and let them see the workers are
all sore.

They're clubbing fellow working men who dare
their thoughts express;

and if Otis has his way, there's sure to be a
mess.

So swell this army, working men, and show them
what we'll do

When all the sons of toil unite in *One Big Union*
true.

We have put the town of Aberdeen [South Dakota] with others
on our map;

And the brass bound thugs of all of them were
handy with the "sap";

But the I.W.W.'s are boys who have no fears

And we'll whip old San Diego if it takes us twenty
years.

Frank Little was quite likely among those who had been clubbed
for expressing their thoughts, since San Diego was part of the south-
western corridor in which Little did a great deal of organizing.

By March 2012 the process of organizing discontent had most
San Diego newspapers raging against the "lawlessness" of the free-

speech fighters. The *San Diego Sun* was an exception, publishing a piece by a San Diego resident who had toured the cells where free-speech fighters were kept, that included the following observation: "The dogs in the city pound are treated better than these men." The next month, Adam R. Sauer, editor of the *San Diego Herald*, the other paper sympathetic to the free-speech fighters, printed prisoners' affidavits, which told of being transported to the desert, beaten, and threatened with death if they dared return to San Diego. On April 15, Sauer was kidnapped, bound, and run out of town.

In May the terror reached new heights. While Emma Goldman was delivering a lecture on Ibsen's *Enemy of the People*, her traveling companion Ben Reitman, a Chicago physician known as the "hobo doctor" or "whorehouse doctor" because he practiced medicine among hoboes and prostitutes and other outcasts of the capitalist system, was taken from his hotel, driven twenty miles out of town, tortured and urinated on. Then he was held down, tarred, and covered in sage brush (apparently no feathers were readily available). In an article for the *Industrial Worker*, Reitman wrote: "with tar from a can [they] traced IWW on my back and a doctor burned the letters in with a lighted cigar." He was forced to run a fourteen- or fifteen-man gauntlet and a cane was shoved up his butt. He was made to kiss the American flag and sing "The Star Spangled Banner." Finally, he was allowed to drag himself away in his vest and underwear. His assailants allowed Reitman to keep his underwear in deference to the possibility of him being seen by "Christian ladies."[3]

On May 31, the *San Francisco Call*, owned by John D. Speckels, who also owned the vigilantes' official organ, the *San Diego Union*, told its readers: "The IWW are disloyal to the government, foes alike of labor, of capital, of organized society. They should not be permitted to preach or teach or practice their hateful doctrines anywhere in the United States."

Western Wobblies were often accused of hating organized society, and at least some eastern Wobblies would not have disagreed with those charges. The centralization practiced by the eastern branch of the union is of course at the core of organized society as we know it. Centralization invariably has a vertical, from-the-top-down structure, which is directly opposed to the western IWW from-the-bottom-out, collectivist structure. To the extent that theory directed his praxis, Frank Little stood with the collectivists. However, he was far more a man of action than a theorist. His organizing strategy before 1915 relied heavily on word of mouth via the hobo grapevine and his own instincts. His knowledge of the hobo jungles, his backyard so to speak, led Frank Little to San Diego. There were jungles near the railroad tracks throughout the West and working stiffs in perpetual motion were constantly moving through them. They would surely have served as relay stations for information. After Missoula, Spokane, and Fresno, Frank Little had a reputation. (Can you imagine the reaction in the jungles when word got around that the hobo agitator had advised the Fresno cops to go on strike?) The hysterical reactions of the San Diego vigilantes show, to a significant degree, fear of a growing radical movement.

## DENVER

The struggle in Denver began when three IWW speakers were arrested on the day after Christmas in 1912. The speakers were jailed and a call for volunteers went out. Over the next few weeks more than forty Wobblies were arrested for speaking to crowds on the street, but those numbers did not satisfy the union leadership. On January 9, 1913, the *Industrial Worker* expressed disappointment at "the apathy of rebels throughout the country in not responding more readily to the call." We can imagine Little waving the paper in the faces of California jungle residents and crying: "See what your fellow workers back east think of you sitting here on your backsides while a fight's going on in Denver. Are we going to let them think we don't give a damn, or are we going to come down on Denver like a swarm of locusts?"

Those Wobblies already in jail were released. They spoke to street crowds again and were duly arrested and re-jailed. By March the struggle was at fever pitch. Frank Little organized freight-train caravans, which started in Taft, California, passed through Bakersfield, Fresno, Stockton, Oakland, San Francisco, Sacramento, and points east before arriving in Denver. Philip S. Foner quotes Ed Nolan, a participant in one of the earliest caravans, as saying: "Upon leaving Oakland a painful sprain was sustained by fellow worker Frank Little, but he will shortly follow with another crew. A sprain is nothing to that indomitable spirit of his."

## WHEATLAND

The Durst Brothers ranch at Wheatland, near Marysville, California, sent out three thousand colorful ads for hop pickers; but hired only half of those who applied, thereby keeping wages low. A worker camp of men, women, and children, who among them spoke twenty-seven different languages, had no toilets in the field and no garbage disposal. Temperatures routinely topped one hundred degrees, but workers were forced to walk a mile for a drink of water. Carlton H. Parker's investigation after the Wheatland riot occurred found that a hop picker's daily pay could be as high as $1.80 or as low as 70 cents. Parker took his figures at random from the ranch's account books. Durst admitted prohibiting groceries from Wheatland stores being brought in to the camp. He owned half of the general food stores available to workers.

A riot broke out on August 3, 1913, but Frank Little would probably have been on the scene well before then. He had already been working with agricultural laborers for three years, and at the 1914 IWW national convention he proposed that a communication network be set up for the express purpose of organizing agricultural workers. Like San Diego, Wheatland was part of a Southern California area in which he did a considerable amount of agitating and organizing. The farm workers respected Little's dedication to free speech and the IWW's strictly enforced color-blind policy on race. The latter should not be underestimated as during the period in question; to my knowledge, no other comparably broad-based union enforced such a policy.

The riot began when police broke up an IWW outdoor meeting at which Richard "Blackie" Ford and H. D. Suhr were about to speak. During the ensuing violence, a district attorney, deputy sheriff, and two hop pickers were killed. The authorities claimed whoever killed the district attorney was incited by IWW rhetoric, so Ford and Suhr were charged with first-degree murder. The two men were convicted and the IWW launched a campaign against what it called a "judicial crime." The union had nine demands, one of which called for Ford and Suhr being retried and charges dismissed if any crops were to be picked. The AFL endorsed the strike in San Francisco, Sacramento, and Fresno and despite verbal intimidation it spread throughout the state and managed to reduce the crops' total value by about 10 percent.

Philip S. Foner makes a believable case that the hobo jungle in Marysville received almost as much notoriety as the trial. Articles in the *San Francisco Bulletin* and *San Francisco Star* praised the peaceful, calm, orderly, and alcohol-free IWW-organized jungle communities. Even if Frank Little was not directly involved in the Wheatland affair, his prominent role in establishing the kind of jungle communities described in the *Bulletin* and the *Star* is beyond doubt.

## LOS ANGELES

On the day after Christmas in 1913, unemployed workers denouncing starvation amidst plenty held a demonstration at the Los Angeles Plaza. The action took place in an area Frank Little routinely worked in and involved the bottom-dog workers he knew so well. The Plaza demonstration helped set the stage for "General" Charles

E. Kelley, a leader in Coxey's Army, calling for a march on Washington, DC. On February 12, 1914, fifteen hundred unemployed workers, including an IWW contingent, left San Francisco en route to Sacramento and points east. The *Sacramento Bee* labeled the army of unemployed "a gang of thugs, deadbeats, and vagrants" and called for vigilante action against them. Long before reaching their final destination an attack on the marchers by police, deputies, and members of the fire department wielding ax pick handles occurred, which became known as "Bloody Monday." Even though threatened with jail, Helen Keller gave public support to the marchers. The attack put an abrupt and violent end to what might have become a huge movement of the unemployed. Little quite possibly participated in the Los Angeles Plaza demonstration and perhaps the aborted march as well, though he may still have been in Kansas City when the latter took place.

## KANSAS CITY

On January 5, 1914, five organizers were arrested for holding street meetings in Kansas City. Upon hearing of the arrests Little, who was at the time in California, headed east with a contingent of free-speech fighters. The Wobblies followed the usual strategy of pressuring the authorities by overcrowding the jails. This would have been Little's second free-speech action in Kansas City. He had been arrested in October 1911 for speaking to a crowd on the street and was engaged in free-speech activities in that city through December. According to Nigel Sellars, Little "arrived in Oklahoma just after taking part in the Kansas City free-speech fight. Ill at the time, he stayed with a friend, Mrs. Allie L. Cox, in Guthrie, but wrote to *Solidarity*, then the main IWW newspaper, to report on conditions."

Frank Little's leadership in the 1914 Kansas City conflict has been noted by both Melvyn Dubofsky and Philip S. Foner. Little organized a hunger strike and successfully used it as leverage against city authorities. Local newspaper accounts of Little's activities have disappeared. Apparently by 1914 the Kansas City press was ignoring the activities of radicals while giving a good bit of ink to the fears those activities aroused.

## FREE SPEECH AND THE WAR

While the free-speech fights did not interfere with Little's commitment to collectivism, by the end of 1913 the IWW's organizational priorities were causing him to reevaluate his convictions. If the nomadic farm laborers of the West and South were to be organized, a centralized communication network needed to be established. At the 1914 IWW national convention, Little submitted a proposal that sought to establish cooperation among the different locals on a common organizational program in the grain fields. The convention of 1914 was a turning point in Little's career as a Wobbly organizer. It could be said to mark the end of the union's participation in the free-speech struggles, a campaign Little had thrown himself into body and soul. His discontent in the face of the GEB withdrawing its support from such fights must have been substantial. Labor organizer William Z. Foster claims in his autobiography to have won

Little's support during the 1914 convention for his plan, urged on by the success of recent strikes in England, to dissolve the IWW as a labor union and turn it into a propaganda league which would "bore from within" the trade unions and revolutionize them as the syndicalists in France had done. It comes as no surprise that Little would have favored this.

One cannot help wondering if along with Little's popularity among western Wobblies and his outstanding work as an agitator and organizer, another reason for his election to the GEB was to bind him more closely to the IWW power structure. His election would have helped to mend the fissure between the union's eastern and western branches. His admittance to the board would likewise have helped take the sting out of the leadership's abandonment of free-speech fights. In order to be elected he would have needed the support of a significant number of eastern centralists as they held a majority among those members who actually voted.

Whatever strategies may or may not have been involved in Frank Little being elected to the GEB, his commitment to free speech remained unshaken. Frank Little was lynched because of his fierce opposition to the United States entering the war in Europe; his antiwar stance was clearly a free-speech issue. It is routinely observed that Little's opposition to the United States entering the war was not shared by the vast majority of the union's rank and file. In assessing the numbers of those who shared his view, we need first to consider the bigger picture. Six weeks after war had been declared, of the one million men needed to fight, only seventy-three thousand had volunteered. The summons to arms, what President Woodrow Wilson was calling the war "to end all war" and "to make the world safe for democracy," clearly did not create the response the government had hoped for. Congress immediately voted for conscription.

Native Americans were still without the vote, but they were pressured to join the military. "Citizen Indians," Native Americans who had worked government-allotted land for the twenty-five year trust period or who had a "certificate of competency," became subject to the draft. In June, draft registration was required of all Indian males. Protests sprung up on several reservations, including Fort Hall in Idaho, the Navajo agencies in Arizona, and the Goshiute reservation in Utah. The Goshiute resisters claimed, quite correctly, that not being able to vote they were not citizens and only "citizen Indians" were subject to the draft. Eventually, over ten thousand Indian males enlisted. Many of those enlistees came from military-style boarding schools. The "Five Civilized Tribes," which included the Cherokee, Chickasaw, Choctaw, Creek, and Seminole Indians, contributed more than four thousand young men. These numbers are striking when we consider that the American Indian population was just three years short of its smallest number in history: two hundred and fifty thousand people.

That same June, President Woodrow Wilson signed the Espionage Act into law. It contained a clause that made virtually any public opposition to the war a felony, punishable by up to twenty years in prison, "whoever, when the United States is at war, shall willfully cause or attempt to cause insubordination, disloyalty, mutiny, or refusal to duty in the military or naval forces of the United States, or shall willfully obstruct the recruiting or enlistment service of the US." Frank Little's position on the war—stay home and fight your real enemy—was now illegal.

The nation's ruling elite, including J. P. Morgan, the DuPonts, Marcellus Hartley Dodge, and Charles Schwab, were all the while beating the drum for US involvement in the war. In fact, even before officially entering the war, the United States' involvement was considerable. The British liner *Lusitania*, torpedoed and sunk by a German submarine, was said by US authorities to have been carrying no American-produced war-related cargo. But, according to Howard Zinn, it carried "1,248 cases of 3-inch shells, 4,927 boxes of cartridges (1,000 rounds in each box), and 2,000 more cases of small-arms ammunition. Her manifests were falsified to hide this fact, and the British and American government lied about the cargo." Zinn also informs us that in 1914 a serious recession began in the United States, but by the next year "war orders for the Allies (mostly England) had stimulated the economy and by April, 1917, more than $2 billion worth of goods had been sold to the Allies."

A large enough number of Americans demonstrated their suspicions about and lack of enthusiasm for the war in Europe to cause the government to continue its June offensive. The Department of Justice sponsored an American Protective League, which had units in six hundred cities and towns, and a membership of almost one hundred thousand people, including community leaders, bankers, railroad men, and hotel men. The League searched private mail with impunity. The *Minneapolis Journal* ran an appeal by the Minnesota Commission of Public Safety "for all patriots to join in the suppression of anti-draft and seditious acts and sentiments." Newspaperman George Creel's Commission of Public Information called on citizens to "report the man who spreads pessimistic stories." Despite these orchestrated efforts to suppress antiwar activity, on the day Frank Little was murdered, August 1, 1917, the *New York Herald* observes that in New York City alone ninety of the first hundred draftees claimed exemption.

When war was declared in April 1917, the IWW led by Bill Haywood began to back away from its previous antiwar position, saying instead that the war in Europe and the class war were entirely separate wars. It was a spurious conclusion considering the fortunes being made by the war, fought in large part (especially with regard to body count) by working-class males from all the combatant countries. In his autobiography, Haywood recalls his response when the war in Europe began. "For weeks I could scarcely talk," he wrote. "I could not read, as my mind was fixed on the war." An experienced politico, Haywood immediately saw the conflict's implications and its directives for US capitalists. He had opposed the Spanish-American War, the invasion of the Philippines, and in lectures advised workingmen to avoid "the frenzy of saber-rattling along the Mexican border." He had said, "Let the capitalists fight their own battles. They are only too willing to put workingmen up to be shot at." But now the war in Europe had Haywood ready to take a much softer position.

In 1916, the IWW had adopted a resolution opposing the latest war—and all wars. "We proclaim the anti-military propaganda in time of peace and in time of war, the general strike in all industries." In March 1917, the United States was a month away from officially entering the European struggle, *Solidarity* published a front-page piece, bordered in funeral black and entitled "The Deadly Parallel:"

We, the Industrial Workers of the World, in Convention assembled, hereby reaffirm our adherence to the principles of industrial unionism and we dedicate ourselves to the
unflinching, unfaltering prosecution of the struggle for the abolition of wage slavery, and the realization of our ideal in industrial democracy. With the European war in conquest and
exploitation raging and destroying lives, class consciousness
and the unity of workers, and ever-growing agitation for military preparedness clouding the main issues, and delaying the realization of our ultimate aim with patriotic and, therefore,
capitalistic aspirations, we openly declare ourselves determined
opponents of all nationalistic sectionalism, or patriotism, and
militarism preached and supported by our enemy, the capitalist
class. We condemn all wars, and for the prevention of such, we
proclaim an anti-militarist propaganda in time of peace, thus
promoting Class Solidarity among the workers of the entire
world, and in time of war, the General Strike in all industries."
According to Haywood, the resolution was "formulated from
the Lenin resolution at the Zimmerwald Conference.

Inspired by his disdain for AFL president Samuel Gompers,
Haywood had "The Deadly Parallel" distributed as a leaflet by the
thousands. That decision would later haunt him. The recently
passed Espionage Act made "The Deadly Parallel" illegal and beyond First Amendment protection. Haywood stopped distribution
of the leaflet. Frank Little responded by demanding an "increase"
of its distribution and that of other antiwar literature. Writing to
Haywood, Little said: "I for one, by God, will not keep still. I want
to see our papers express themselves. If we fight, let us fight for
freedom. Now is the time for us to take a stand." Haywood replied,

"My advice in this crisis is a calm head and cool judgment. Talk is not the thing needed now."

For the moment let us confine ourselves to the free-speech aspects of Little and Haywood's disagreement. Little appears to have been ready to seize what in his eyes was a teaching moment and run with it—"I want to see our papers express themselves"—and Haywood is closing up shop because the time is not right—"talk is not the thing needed now"—though he offers no reasons why. The latter's position is fixed: say nothing, stay "calm" but make no attempt to explain the fruits of your "cool judgment." Haywood seems to be stuck between gears. Flooded by letters asking his advice about whether or not to register for the draft, he took "no official stand . . . believing that the individual member was the best judge of how to act on the question." Suddenly, the man known as Mister IWW, who normally had the final word on all important decisions, was speechless. Ethically speaking, saying each member had to make his own decision was a sound, even necessary, move. But by relinquishing his influence, Big Bill helped give free reign to a virtual forest fire of pro-war hysteria emanating from Washington, DC, and Wall Street. Of course, it could be justifiably argued that not transgressing the law allowed the union to continue organizing through other means.

Until the US war in Vietnam, anything like genuine free speech was, for all practical purposes, suspended during time of war. If the suspension had been based on the fear of loose lips sinking ships, the policy might be defendable. But during World War One it was not. The brunt of its enforcement landed on anyone who opposed or even seriously questioned US involvement in the war. So far as Frank Little was concerned, opposing US involvement in the European war was like opposing the rule of the Steel Trust. On August 4, 1916, speaking to a crowd in Virginia, Minnesota, Little was quoted by the *Duluth Herald Tribune* as saying: "The laws of the state and the nation are made by men controlled by the Steel Trust." We have already noted the Trust's enormous vested interest in US involvement in the war.

By his own light, Little was still attempting to educate the American worker as he had done in Missoula, Spokane, Fresno, Kansas City, the Mesabi Iron Range, and so many other places. He was attempting to help people consider views they had not before encountered or, perhaps out of fear, sought to avoid. His commitment to the task was unshakable. Not long before Little was murdered, he told *Solidarity* editor Ralph Chaplin he would rather "take a firing squad" than back down on the war.

Newspaperman W. W. Wallister testified during the IWW conspiracy trial that in a speech Little delivered on July 31, 1917, he had referred to US soldiers in Europe as "armed thugs" and "Pershing's yellow legs." Both epithets fall under the umbrella of free speech if the term is to have any authentic meaning, for if the most offensive statements are not protected by free speech, what real value has the concept apart from its propaganda value for the status quo? When we examine the epithets from Little's point of view, a logic emerges readily enough—unsettling as that logic may be to conventional patriotic sentiments. The troops in question had been armed by a government that was run, for all practical purposes, by the Steel Trust. From Little's perspective, the troops were acting the same as the armed thugs who had served the Trust so faithfully during labor conflicts. As "armed thug"-soldiers, they were fighting for capitalists who had continuously opposed the so-called thug when he was a worker. In Wobbly lingo, "yellow legs" referred to "mounted police or the United States Cavalry," both of whom were deployed against rebellious workers. They were characterized as yellow because a man on horseback has a decided physical advantage over a man on foot. The rider's legs would be what the man on foot saw as he tried to defend himself or dodge both horse and truncheon; therefore, Little uses the term "yellow legs" based on the experiences of striking workers. In a more ideological sense, though for Little it may well have been a personal affront, the soldiers had given up the class war for the safer capitalist war—safer in the sense of it being legitimate in the eyes of the law, the capitalist press, and well-financed civic groups that praised enlistees to the sky while scolding and persecuting striking workers.[4]

The money, time, and force expended by the government to orchestrate support for the war is sufficient evidence for discounting the argument that antiwar sentiments were held by only a tiny minority. We have seen that the demographics argue against any such view. But whatever the number of those who believed as Little did, historian Mark Leier recounts a more pressing democratic and moral concern: "No serious historian today believes that WWI was fought by Britain, France, and their allies to preserve democracy or end all war. Yet millions of people were told precisely that in order to secure their compliance. . . . Morality requires that those who fought and died know the real reason for the fighting." For this principle alone, Frank Little's allegiance to free speech stands justified.

# CHAPTER THREE
# Iron Miners, Harvest Hands, and Oil Workers

## THE MESABI STRIKE OF 1913

From the beginning, the mines of the Mesabi Iron Range had been administered in a rigorously anti-union fashion. The bosses quickly stamped out any sign of unions or strikes. Located in northeastern Minnesota, about sixty miles inland northwest of a thriving Duluth, the range was the richest iron ore mining center on the planet. Iron ore was first discovered on the Mesabi Range in 1890, and, as Philip S. Foner put it, "settlements sprung up in the wilderness surrounding open pits and mine shafts, and in time came villages and towns bearing the names of Mt. Iron, McKinley, Biwabik, Virginia, Eveleth, Hibbing, Nishwauk, Keewaitin, and Bovey." An immigrant population of more than thirty nationalities poured into these towns, all of them within a distance of roughly sixty miles. English, Irish, Scotch, French, and Finns were prominent among the first arrivals. "By 1910, there were at least 35 different nationality groups on the Range of sufficient size to be easily identifiable" while a "smattering" of at least ten other nationalities were also in residence. In those days iron miners worked mostly underground. The most demanding physical tasks were assigned to the foreign-born while operating machines and other skilled work went to English speakers, Scandinavians (their numbers and resultant connections rendered them exempt to the foreign-born rule), and a few "native-born sons of immigrants."

As the twentieth century began, large and powerful companies owned the mines. John D. Rockefeller took over Lake Superior Consolidated Iron Mines when the Merritt brothers could no longer pay their debts. Andrew Carnegie was, of course, another prominent player. By 1902, the Carnegie-Oliver Company was mining 60 percent of the total range production. Six years later, US Steel owned about 75 percent of the total reserve tonnage in iron ore. The other mine owners were subsidiaries of steel and furnace companies like Oliver. US Steel could be aptly described as a monopolist's monopoly; the first billion-dollar corporation, it controlled two-thirds of the nation's steel production.

It is generally held that the IWW's first significant offensive against the Steel Trust came in 1916. But under Frank Little's leadership, the Wobblies engaged the Trust three years earlier in the summer of 1913. We find the roots of that conflict in a 1907 strike led by the Western Federation of Miners (WFM). As it happens, at the WFM convention that same year, Little supported the IWW direct-action agenda and opposed a narrow electoral approach to politics. The WFM split with the IWW. Little stayed with the latter and was subsequently expelled by the former.

The miners' living accommodations on the Mesabi Range were minimal at best. Most of these accommodations consisted of one-room dwellings with beds along the walls that were constantly in use by day and night shift workers. A couple, their children, and two or three boarders all lived under one roof. The work was seasonal; the mines virtually closed three to five months a year because of the cold. By 1905, the full-time residents of mine towns such as Hibbing, Virginia, and Chisholm, Minnesota, had well-paved streets lined with trees, electric street lighting, excellent houses, and libraries. The glaring contrast between this style of living and the manner in which the miners and their families were forced to live must certainly have played a role in the miners' unrest.

The workers' leaders were largely Finnish radical intellectuals who had first discovered socialist and anarchist ideas at temperance halls and workers' clubs in their home country, though the socialists would soon establish their own halls in opposition to the temperance movement. A concerted organizing campaign by the WFM, under the leadership of Teofila Petriella, and assisted by Vincent St. John, led to a strike being called on July 20, 1907. The president of US Steel's offices in Oliver, Minnesota, Thomas F. Cole, was told to take a stand against the strikers. Special deputies were employed and instructed to use any methods necessary to break the strikes. Company agents and gunmen came pouring into the Range. Local merchants were expected to deny credit to strikers.

Finnish socialist halls served as meeting places for the strike. A Duluth *News Tribune* headline mixed fear and hyperbole: "Blood Red Flag Flaunted by The Federation Strikers. Finns March Through Streets of Sparta, Led by Amazon Bearing the Emblem of Anarchy." The identity of said "Amazon" is not disclosed; the accompanying photograph shows a woman carrying a flag.

The Duluth *News Tribune* reported Mother (Mary) Jones defiantly challenged the deputies to "Shoot & Be Damned." In less than a month, carloads of strikebreakers, scabs to the strikers, arrived to work in the mines. They were Eastern European immigrants, newly arrived in the United States at the Steel Trust's expense and consequently already in debt to the companies. Oftentimes they did not know a strike was in progress. These new arrivals and the company's strong-arm tactics defeated the strikers by mid-September. The Duluth *News Tribune* had prophesized that victory on August 19: "Army of Deputies Overawe the Western Federation of Miners."[1]

Of the nearly three dozen nationalities that participated in the strike, the Finns paid the highest price. Eighteen percent of the Oliver Iron Mining Company labor force was Finnish before 1907, but only 8 percent remained after 1907. By 1908 the WFM had disappeared from the Mesabi Range, and the AFL Minnesota State Federation declined an opportunity to organize there.

In 1913, Frank Little led an ore dockworkers' strike that has been all but ignored by history. Even historians of the IWW like

Philip S. Foner, Joseph R. Conlin, and Patrick Renshaw make no mention of the 1913 conflict; nor does Big Bill Haywood's autobiography. Melvyn Dubofsky briefly mentions Little being kidnapped and rescued but does not deal with the strike's contribution to a major labor offensive in the northern Minnesota, Wisconsin, and Michigan mining area.

The summer of 1913 saw considerable labor unrest on the Mesabi Range, as well as a major strike of copper miners, led by the WFM, in Calumet, Michigan. That same summer, efforts to organize farm laborers were suppressed in Minot, North Dakota. The first significant labor conflict of the season was reported by the Duluth *News Tribune* on July 22, 1913, sparked by miners' demands to be paid on the tenth of every month instead of on the twentieth. The demand apparently shocked the company, and it sent in a security force from Two Harbors to protect company property. The *News Tribune* reassured its readers that the strikers were "orderly" and "no trouble is anticipated." The newspaper makes no mention of Little being beaten on that same day, but the incident appears in Gene Lantz's timeline. Four days later, fifteen thousand Calumet miners went on strike. When the union drove away the sheriff's deputies, he called for help from state troops. After investigating the situation, a team of state militia commanders ruled that troops were not warranted.

That same July 26, fifteen Eveleth miners who had been trapped underground filed a damage suit asking for $100 for each hour of their ordeal. The next day, the Calumet strike made front-page headlines at the *News Tribune* when a local general store that had stopped allowing strikers to buy on credit was burned down, and the owners accused strike sympathizers of arson. Two companies of state troopers were immediately dispatched. On July 30, at least seventy Calumet striking miners came to Duluth looking for work. The next day, three strikers were arrested and the state militia had to save outnumbered deputies from a threatening mob. When the residents of a Hungarian boarding house at the Wolverine mine fought sheriff deputies, they deployed hot water, red pepper spray, and household utensils against the state's revolvers and bayonets. The WFM pledged to do "everything possible" for those arrested.

On the night of July 31, 1913, two Great Northern Railroad ore trains collided. Thirty miners were thrown into ore pockets; three of them were killed and four hundred and fifty of their fellow workers immediately went on strike. Great Northern countered by offering a raise of fifteen cents per ten-hour workday and the introduction of safety appliances. A mass meeting of Allouez strikers was held at Woodman Hall in Superior, Wisconsin, at which Frank Little was the featured speaker. As reported by the News Tribune, Little "controlled the situation and appeared to hold the faith and confidence of the men." He read a general strike proclamation, but no action was taken because an insufficient number of strikers were present to make it official. Little told the crowd: "The company has admitted it is losing $50,000 a day. Now is the time for you to hold out. You will not lose. There is plenty of work in the harvest fields. Demand an 8 hour day . . . Duluth is with us and I hope Two Harbors [Michigan] and Ashland [Wisconsin] and other ports will join hands in our fight."

By telling the striking miners about the available harvest work,

Little was offering a viable alternative to the strikers' common plight of being forced by economic circumstances to ratify unacceptable terms. For some, if not most, the opportunity to work in the sunshine and open air rather than underground must have sounded pretty good. A Duluth *News Tribune* reporter spoke with Little, who said he eventually hoped to call a strike which would affect all sailors of the Great Lakes and workers on the docks as well as the lumberyards and mills.

Little headed the committee that presented the company's offer to the strikers. The workers voted to hold out, and the company rescinded the offer of a pay raise and safety appliances. Some of the strikers blamed Little for their loss of what would have been gains, saying if he had not convinced them to reject the company's proposal they would have taken it and returned to work. On August 3, the *News Tribune* told its readers the strike had thus far "tied up 13 steamers for 10 to 48 hours."

Three days later, the paper announced both Mother Jones's arrival in Calumet, and the US attorney general Walter B. Palmer's order to the Department of Labor to investigate labor conditions in copper country. On August 7, a front-page, bold type, black-bordered headline read: "IWW CANNOT MAKE A PATERSON OF DULUTH." The statement below proclaimed that strikers'had no more right to break a contract they "voluntarily" consented to than the company did. The issue, according to the *News Tribune*, was not a matter of strikebreaking but of honest labor living up to its agreements. Given the economic situation of newly arrived immigrants, the great mass of whom spoke no English and were routinely brought to America under false pretenses (promises of good pay and a generally easy life), the term voluntary consent rings particularly hollow.

According to A. W. M'Gonagle, president of the docks, more than 80 percent of the workers "want to continue to work" and have been intimidated by a few strangers who arrived on the scene with "the avowed purpose of causing trouble." The *News Tribune* clearly placed Frank Little at the head of those troublemakers, since he was known to be the driving force behind the strikers rejecting the company's offer. A comic sketch of a huge, booted foot ("Public Opinion") stepping on a snake ("IWW Agitator") over the caption: "crushing the life out of a poisonous snake" was printed on the front page August 8. That same day the paper ran a bold type message: "DULUTH POLICE HAVE SITUATION IN HAND."

The same issue includes the story of IWW local president, James P. Cannon, reporting Frank Little missing. Cannon had been "diligently" looking for him since Wednesday night, August 6. He said, "It looks like a case of kidnapping. Little left Allouez about nine o'clock with Duluth as his destination. Since that hour we have heard nothing from him." Several Wobblies and strikers thought Little had been "slugged" and his body dumped in the bay. Others thought he'd been arrested and "railroaded" out of town.

Cannon and Little were old friends. James P. Cannon came from a long line of Irish nationalists of the Robert Emmet persuasion. James's father, John, had moved from group to group—first, the Knights of Labor, then the Populists, and later yet the Bryanites—before becoming a socialist. At age sixteen, John's son got involved in socialist politics during the Haywood-Pettibone-

Moyer murder trial. James dropped out of school and dove into radical politics.

A final noteworthy item in the *News Tribune*, August 8 issue, reported a coroner's jury declaring Great Northern Railroad indirectly responsible for the fatal accident that had set off the strike. The verdict was based on "alleged negligence of switchmen clinging to sides of ore cars instead of standing on top, where signals to the engineer can be plainly seen." Inadequate safety gears made a switchman's movements an extremely risky affair.

James P. Cannon was in the news again the following day as he and one of his aides came to blows with Oliver Mining Company police. Wobblies questioned at their headquarters, located at 907 West Superior Street in Duluth, feared Little had "met with a mishap." Joseph Bauer was quoted as saying Little had been "shanghaied and is now bound down the lakes on an ore carrier." He went on to say: "Little's disappearance is too small an incident to check a movement as great as ours. The IWW has a thousand Littles. When one falls, another stands ready to step into the breach." Railroad and dock officials called the disappearance "a fine piece of horseplay" intended to gain public sympathy for the IWW and the strikers. The following description of Frank Little was circulated: "5 feet 10 inches tall, artificial left eye, scar on forehead, dark-brown moustache. Light complexion, wearing brown suit and black slouch hat when last seen."

The August 10 issue of the *News Tribune* ran an interview with an unnamed "Duluthian," a former Wobbly, who said: "Logic and sound thought are not required of an I.W.W. leader. Harangue and fault finding with no suggestion of constructiveness are essentials [to IWW organizing]." The average IWW members "imagine themselves ill used by society and want the satisfaction of belonging to somebody or something that proposes to tear down the existing order of things."

That same day, sheriff's deputies were reported to be standing guard at 2:30 a.m. in front of a farmhouse near Holyoke, Minnesota, in which Frank Little was believed to be held captive. IWW leader Erick Erickson planned on surrounding the house with fellow Wobblies and keeping a vigil until morning when he would ask to see and talk with Little.

Earlier that same night, at 11:10 p.m., James P. Cannon had ordered twenty Wobblies to board a Great Northern train for Holyoke. He gave instructions that they communicate with Little; if such was not possible, the men were to contact the Duluth headquarters for further instructions.

On August 11, Little was rescued from his abductors. The story, as reported by the Duluth *News Tribune*, goes like this: About a mile from Joseph W. Getty's farm, Erickson turned over his command to W. I. Fisher of Minneapolis and returned to Holyoke, three miles away, to call a posse. Fisher crept up on the long deserted farmhouse (Getty had moved into town and become a bricklayer) and discovered a tar-paper shanty in which Little was being held. Meanwhile, Erickson obtained a warrant to arrest the "supposed" abductors and search the premises, but he could not obtain the services of town constable William Sweltzer, who claimed he was too sick to leave his bed and thus unable to do his duty. After "much pleading" on Erickson's part, Justice of the Peace H. E. McCuskey, who had issued the warrant, deputized a local Wobbly named Weller. Erickson and

Weller returned to Getty's farm under sanction of the law. When one of "the tallest" of Frank's abductors saw the jig was up he cried out, "You can have Little but you won't arrest me," and started to run. Erickson pointed a gun at him, but Little said: "Boys, no gun play. Let them go." Shots were fired, but the kidnappers escaped.

Upon his return to Duluth, Little made the following statement to the *News Tribune*:

> I was stepping from an Allouez car at Belknap Street and Tower Avenue in Superior on Wednesday night when five men ordered me into an automobile. At the RR crossing tower of the Great Northern Railroad I was ordered out. Three men accompanied me as I was taken aboard a train. No answer was given when I inquired about my destination. We arrived in Holyoke at shortly after 10 o'clock Thursday morning. They took me to a hotel conducted by A. E. Erickson [not the IWW leader Erickson] I was locked in a room with one of the special detectives. After breakfast the men ordered me to get up and follow them.

When asked about his time on the farm, Little replied, "There is little to say about the four days on Getty's farm. I was not abused and given plenty to eat."

A drawing of the "ore dock strike" working like a boomerang against an "IWW agitator" in a top hat and suit, with the caption: "Boomerang!" appeared in the August 12 *News Tribune*. The same issue quoted docks president M'Gonagle calling the strike "a thing of the past."

Amidst news about the demise of the ore dock strike, Minot, North Dakota, citizens were reported to have attacked Wobblies attempting to organize migratory farm laborers for "alleged insults to the American flag." Wobblies were arrested, and crowds of "citizens, many of them armed" threatened to invade the jail but were dispersed with the fire department's help.

Despite the company's six-year campaign against them, Finnish workers were still strong enough in number that speeches were delivered in Finnish as well as English. On August 13, Allouez Management promised the strikers a raise of a dime a day, but barred Finnish strikers from reemployment. The Duluth *Weekly Herald* announced that the movement of ore on the Mesabi dock had returned to its "normal rate." IWW agitation was now confined to the Superior strike. As far as the company was concerned, it had triumphed, but Frank Little, did not concur. He told the *News Tribune*, "The IWW is always on strike and stays that way until concessions demanded by strikers are granted." He was also quoted as saying he had "several good things to tell the strikers, but the time was not ripe yet." About whether or not the strikers should accept the company's latest offer, he said, "The IWW will not counsel the men either to go back or stay out. That is a question for them to settle, not us. Already a number of IWW members are working on the docks there and when the time is ripe they will do the work the organization assigns to them." Despite the union's policy of neutrality, in a speech to a large group of strikers Little advised them to reject Great Northern's offer. It was, instead, accepted. His actions were consistent with his refusal to concede defeat, a fact that amazed and annoyed the press.

Thanks to the Duluth *News Tribune*, the 1913 strike offers us more of Frank Little's words than any other single action, with the possible exception of the 1916 Mesabi conflict. If he was "beaten up by company goons and left unconscious in the gutter," as Gene Lantz reports, a full nine days before the Great Northern strike began, Little must have already been at work agitating.

In an effort to better understand the threat Little posed, we need to take a closer look at Little's speeches to strikers and remarks to the press. In his August 1 speech at Woodman Hall, Little took an important step in forging a united front between iron miners and harvest hands, as well as offering otherwise trapped workers an escape route when he told the strikers there was "plenty of work in the harvest fields." He was already playing a considerable role in IWW efforts to organize harvest hands. The Wobblies had something of a monopoly in that sphere since the other unions believed those workers to be un-organizable. He concluded his talk with a call for worker solidarity among all the region's ports. In his comments to the press, Little spoke of the general strike he hoped eventually to call.

The *News Tribune* credited Frank Little with single handedly swaying the strikers to reject Great Northern's first offer. The paper had, after all, reported the blame some strikers laid on him when said offer was rescinded. One cannot help wondering whether Frank believed what the press said about him and, if so, what effect that belief might have had on him. Would thinking one had that degree of power over more than five hundred men decrease one's respect toward those men? When strikers held him responsible for the offer being rescinded, did he think: *So now I'm the villain? Something goes wrong, and the boss is immediately off the hook?* Or did he see the Duluth *News Tribune*, in its role as a Great Northern supporter, employing the comments of a few strikers as part of a divide-and-conquer strategy so often used by power in defense of its interests?

The size of the 1913 strike and sensationalism of Frank Little's disappearance make it difficult to comprehend why those events have been all but ignored by IWW historians. We have seen the scope of Wobbly activity during the summer of 1913 was not limited to the ore dockworkers' strike. By August of that year the IWW had been made illegal in Minot, North Dakota, and Little's Woodman Hall speech would certainly have contributed to Minot officials' fear of escalated Wobbly activity. The prospect of Wobbly-inspired iron-miners-turned-harvest-hands invading a wheat-producing giant like North Dakota caused the capitalist class to circle up their wagons and dig in for a fight.

Before we turn to the 1916 conflict, certain aspects of the 1913 struggle still need to be addressed. First, to what extent did the much larger WFM-led copper miners' strike in Calumet aid or hinder the IWW-led ore dockworkers' strike, and how did the former affect Frank's approach to the latter? The size and violence of the Calumet strike, so thoroughly covered by the Duluth press, almost certainly played a prominent role in A. W. M'Gonagle's highly visible conciliatory gestures towards the ore dock strikers and their families. Unlike the Calumet officials who quickly resorted to violence in their efforts to suppress the strike, M'Gonagle presented himself as a friend of the worker and enemy of outside agitators. His approach offers an interesting contrast with the far tougher stance of the Duluth *News Tribune*. The newspaper's position may well have caused those readers not directly involved in the conflict to side with the employers; the Calumet strike would surely have served as a source of inspiration to the strikers and their support-ers. After all, it had managed to take more than fifteen thousand miners out of harness and bring the working conditions of copper miners, and by extension miners generally, to the attention of the public as well as that of the federal government. Perhaps the Calumet conflict inspired a sense of rivalry in the hobo agitator born of his desire to prove to himself and others that he had made the right decision in leaving the WFM for the IWW. We have no reason to believe his commitment to the miners union had not been every bit as strong as his later allegiance to the Wobblies. His decision in 1907 to side with the IWW must have been an ex-tremely difficult one, so why wouldn't a spur to competition have fuelled his work in the ore dock strike?

Second, the press coverage of the conflict repeatedly speaks of "citizens" vigorously opposing IWW agitators. The xenophobic sentiments at work in the press' use of the title citizen need clarifi-cation if we are to fairly assess the conditions under which Wobbly organizing efforts took place. The majority of the miners and farm laborers were not citizens. They were either newly immigrated to the United States or constantly on the move and without a stable address—or both. The miners were overwhelmingly foreign-born while the harvest laborers' most common characteristic was a no-madic life. Their non-citizen status made harvest hands and miners easy targets for the xenophobic. The *News Tribune* cartoon men-tioned above makes it quite clear that the "public opinion" boot stepping on the snake "IWW agitator" contains "citizens."

Third, we need to consider how the strike's outcome, a defeat, at least for the moment, affected Frank Little as an organizer. As the chief IWW leader of the strike, so far as union headquarters was concerned, he would have been held responsible for its failure. On May 22, the hobo agitator had been jailed for conspiracy to riot in Peoria, Illinois, during an unsuccessful free-speech fight. As he was in charge of the ore dock strike, its impact upon him was no doubt more pronounced than the free-speech defeat; but sustaining two losses in so short a time after an impressive, albeit short-lived, series of free-speech victories may offer a clue as to why Frank Little refused to concede defeat in 1913. The defeats served to stiffen his will to resist and strengthened his allegiance to his "always on strike" policy. The record shows he was not given to back pedaling.

Fourth, as economist Paul Brissenden mentions, Little had a policy of "always inaugurating sabotage"; consequently, his remarks about workers already employed on the docks being ready to do the union's bidding when the time was ripe may well have been veiled threats of future sabotage. Or, he may have been responding to M'Gonagle having said the "strike was a thing of the past." In either case, his statements of August 13 leave no doubt the struggle was anything but over so far as Frank Little was concerned.

Finally, Little's election to the GEB in 1914 probably put an end to the level of individualism he had previously known. It seems likely his problems during the ore dock strike did more to help than hinder his election to the GEB. He had proven himself an effective IWW operative. He had the energy, guts, and savvy it took to move men, but he also had a tendency to go too far. Besides his problems at Mesabi, his taunting of the Fresno police by telling them they should strike probably betrayed to Haywood and others that Little possessed a potentially dangerous, even disruptive, tendency. As a member of the Board, Little would be snug under Big Bill Haywood's heavy wing, decidedly outnumbered by eastern Wobblies, and thereby far less capable of seriously rocking the boat.

## THE MESABI STRIKE OF 1916

In his autobiography, Big Bill Haywood ranks the 1916 Minnesota iron miners strike as "a great event in the history of the Industrial Workers of the World," even though three strikers being convicted of murder darkened his memory of the event. The strike began at the Silver Mine in Aurora, Minnesota. The workers' grievances were long established. The owners of the Aurora mine, like all the iron properties, lived back east and workers were recruited from European villages with promises of "high wages and an easy life" in the United States.

Beginning in 1900, a seventy-two-hour workweek was reduced to forty-eight hours over a period of twelve years. But reduced hours brought speed-up requirements. Shortly after the ten-hour day took effect, miners complained that two men were now supposed to complete the work twice their number had done before. The eight-hour workday brought further demands. In their personal correspondence, miners spoke their minds: "We are driven more than we were before. . . . The work expected in ten hours must now be completed in eight." Despite these demands, workers' daily wages, $2.40 for miners and $2.12 for laborers, had not risen since 1909 even though company profits had gone through the roof. Howard Zinn points out that in 1916 alone, US Steel raked in $348 million in profits. Industrialists and political leaders spoke of "prosperity as if it were classless," but the salaries of iron miners did not rise.

In a Report of Mayors and Union Conference, a Chisholm miner of fourteen years experience speaks, in "broken English," of not being able to clothe his wife and seven children like the "nice American" ladies and children on monthly paychecks that ranged from fifty-nine to seventy dollars. "Where am I going to get money? I can't get it working or nothing." Officials discovered that "earnings for many contract miners were often considerably less than Two ($2.00) dollars a day."

In addition to inadequate wages, working conditions for Aurora miners were particularly deplorable. Haywood describes men being "compelled to drag timber through places so small that they had to get down on all fours in the slush and mud to drag the heavy timber to the places where they were working."

On May 13, 1916, an *Industrial Worker* headline, "Steel Slaves Awakening," introduced an appeal from a Virginia, Minnesota, Wobbly urging the IWW to send organizers to the Range. The ensuing strike's leaders were from Italy, Russia, and Bulgaria. The Finns were no longer dominant, though their Socialist halls still served as strike headquarters in the Range towns.

The first IWW organizers to arrive in Virginia were James Gilday, chairman of the organization committee of the Agricultural Workers Organization (AWO), Sam Scarlett, Arthur Boose, Joe Schmidt, and Carlo Tresca. Scarlett was first in command, with Tresca second and Schmidt third.[2]

Philip Foner tells us that on June 2, Joe Greeni, an underground worker at the St. James mine near Aurora who was insulted by the wages he had just received, "threw down his pick," quit his job with the cry: "To hell with such wages!" The rest of the underground workers on that shift followed suit. Greeni and some of his comrades marched from site to site of the Aurora mines, crying: "We've been robbed long enough. It's time to strike." By June 4, all of Aurora's mines were closed and every worker on strike. Wobblies spoke to capacity crowds in several languages. Officially, the IWW was acting in an "advisory capacity only," yet several Wobblies were quite active in the strike's early stages. Once the action began, it quickly spread to the Cayuna and Vermilion iron districts, and soon some sixteen thousand men were involved.

On that same June 4, the Duluth *News Tribune* gave a front-page account of a Preparedness Parade in Chicago that drew 230,214 participants and took eleven hours and thirty minutes to pass through its route, singing, whistling, and humming patriotic songs. An observer was quoted as saying there was "no way of telling a millionaire from a clerk, except by personal recognition." Among the propertied classes a defensive attitude permeated the air.

Miners from Aurora, Biwabik, Eveleth, and Gilbert arrived in Virginia on June 14 for the purpose of closing its mines. The next day, xenophobic statements by President Woodrow Wilson graced the *News Tribune*'s front page. The president said, "foreign-born citizens of the United States are trying to levy political blackmail and undermine the influence of the national government." He continued: "There is disloyalty active in the United States and it must be absolutely crushed. It proceeds from a minority, a very small minority, but a very active and subtle minority." The IWW must surely have considered itself a prime target of Wilson's charge.

The next day, the *News Tribune* reports a large "Spirit of 76" parade sponsored by the Elks occurred. Father A. B. C. Dunne told a crowd of twelve thousand people, "There should be no room for differences of creed or religion in America." A full page in that edition is devoted to the Elks "New Americanism" and readers assured that "All members [are] patriotic."

On June 16, the Duluth *News Tribune* quoted Sam Scarlett as telling fifteen thousand strikers at the Finnish hall in Virginia, Minnesota, to kill three company gunmen for every striker killed. A Virginia citizens committee quickly responded by denouncing the IWW. The newspaper reported that one committee member, R. J. Montagne, told the press "Industrial Wreckers of the World is a more fitting name [for the IWW]. They leave a trail of blood and crime everywhere they go. Something must be done to rid the city of them." Scarlett replied that the IWW would not leave town. "Even if they are powerful enough to drive us out, it will only be as far as Duluth, from where we'll come back and come back strong." An article from a nameless source provided extended statements that said, "Unorganized labor is being paid 35 or 40 percent more than a year ago," and that there were more jobs available than men to fill them. The latter assertion was intended to counter union charges of companies advertising far more work than was in fact available so as to create a labor surplus and keep wages low.

IWW enemies must have rejoiced at the June 17 *News Tribune*'s announcement of Wobbly organizers having failed to rouse workers in Eveleth or Hibbing. The former article was titled "Miners Listen Good Naturedly for a While, Then Yawn, Get Up and Go Home," while the latter piece asserts that IWW agitators's attempts "to induce miners to quit work was received with a laugh." The paper assured its readers that the Virginia strike was not growing, and laborers deplored IWW "anarchist" views. The following day, the union was said to have been condemned by municipal officials throughout the range. The newspaper informed its readers that even a reportedly pro-labor editor like E. A. Koen of Biwabik "bitterly denounced the tactics of the strikers," writing, "Coercion cannot be tolerated in America. . . . Agitators saw an opportunity to fleece their fellows. They are doing it neatly."

As chronicled by the *News Tribune*, the events of June 21 and 22 made a mockery of Hibbing and Eveleth miners alleged disinterest in the IWW's message. On June 21, twelve thousand Eveleth workers voted to strike at a meeting led by Scarlett, Schmidt, and Tresca. The next day, one thousand striking miners battled citizens and police in the streets of Hibbing. The battle was said to have begun when strikers marched under a red banner rather than the stars and stripes. Those same two days saw the arrest of Virginia Wobbly Frank Malna for preventing a worker from going to his job, and the beginning of the trial of thirteen Wobblies accused of threatening and throwing rocks at scabs. The defense called the case a "frame up" as strikers were not armed and did not resist the police. Virginia miners "voted for a general walkout." Starting from Virginia, and led by Scarlett, Tresca, and Schmidt, strikers marched from town to town urging other miners to join them. On June 21 they combined with Hibbing strikers and were

"several thousand strong." They carried banners reading: "Gunmen Beware—Keep Away"; "Citizens, We Want Your Sympathy";
"One Big Union, One Big Enemy." They carried a red flag, which
brought forth vigilantes, and a riot broke out in which many strikers were injured. The following day, another march resulted in the
participants being attacked, but this time they fought back. The
Agricultural Workers Organization was already employing a fight-
back policy, overturning a nonviolent praxis of which Frank Little
had been a leading exponent. John Alar, a Croatian miner and father of three, was killed when guards opened fire. No one was arrested for the crime.

On June 24, Haywood sent a telegram to Carlo Tresca saying
"Frank Little is leaving here [Chicago] tonight for the range. . . .
There is a big territory there to cover. If you need more organizers
after Little arrives, let me know, and I will send the best material
we've got." He included thirty-six dollars to cover two weeks union
expenses. That same day the strikers issued the following six demands: first, an eight-hour day in all Range mines to be timed from
when miner enters the mine until he leaves; second, a pay rate of
$2.75 a day for open-pit miners and $3.00 to $3.50 for under-
ground work, with the higher pay going to those who worked on
wet ground; third, bimonthly paydays; fourth, immediate pay for
quitting miners; fifth, abolition of Saturday night shift; and sixth,
abolition of contract system. The miners did not ask the company
to recognize the union, only that "the men be given a reasonable
wage and that certain forms of work be abolished."

Carlo Tresca and Sam Scarlett were charged with criminal libel
for having carried a banner that read—"Murdered by Oliver Gun-

men"—during John Alar's funeral procession on June 26. Frank Little arrived in Hibbing on June 30, the same day Marxist George Andreytchine was taken into custody under a deportation warrant. Andreytchine, a Bulgarian civil engineer, worked for Carnegie-Oliver and had played a prominent role in putting the strike on its feet. The *News Tribune* credits Little and Tresca with "pacifying" a large group of strikers who were ready to force the authorities to release Andreytchine. That same day's news also contained a report of Governor Burnquist ordering Sheriff John Meining to disarm all strikers, who now numbered more than five thousand men. Beginning that night, Oliver police, with repeating Winchesters, would be "patrolling mining properties prepared to shoot to kill if any striker steps on mining property." If we assume this order was intended to prevent sabotage, should we likewise assume Frank Little's presence was a primary cause of it being issued? After all, two years earlier the Chicago *Daily News* quoted him as saying, "Wherever I go I inaugurate sabotage among the workers. Eventually the bosses will learn why it is that machinery is spoiled and their workers slowing down." To my knowledge, the IWW is the only US labor union to officially endorse sabotage. The usual strict prohibition against sabotage as a tactic is particularly odd when we consider how routinely companies employed physical violence against striking workers. Sabotage hits an employer's pocketbook and, perhaps, his pride, but it does not put a bullet in him or bash in his head with a billy club.

On July 2, a bold print advertisement called for "200 men to act as Deputy Sheriffs." Applicants were told to apply to Sheriff J. R. Meining. Below this announcement was a report of Carlo Tresca being arrested for "unlawful assemblage and inciting miners to violence." Tresca had spoken of exacting an-eye-for-an-eye vengeance at John Alar's graveside.

On July 4, the *News Tribune*'s front page included a description of the circumstances under which a Duluth deputy sheriff, James ("Jimmie") Myron and a soda pop peddler, Thomas Ladvalla, were killed. Three deputy sheriffs and a special agent for the Picklands-Mather company, Nick Dillon, had attempted to serve a warrant for "blindpigging" (running a speakeasy) at Phillip Marsonovich's home in Biwabik. They were met at the door by Mrs. Marsonovich, who blocked their way with a "long pole." When Deputy Sheriff Edward Schubisky tried to pass by her she struck him on the head with the pole, knocking him to the ground; a fact the reporter said "probably" saved Schubisky's life. A gun battle broke out. Myron was shot through the throat. Ladvalla was killed by a stray bullet to the body.

In his autobiography, Bill Haywood refers to Nick Dillon as a "notorious character." Philip S. Foner says the men trying to enter her house by force began "to abuse Mrs. Marsonovich and a number of Montenegrin boarders," violence ensued and "a deputized mine guard" from Duluth, James C. Myron, was killed as was Thomas Ladvalla, a "soda pop deliverer." Everyone in the house was arrested. In Virginia, about twenty miles away, Sam Scarlett, Carlo Tresca, Joe Schmidt, James Gilday, Frank Little, Leo Stark, Frank Russell, and some other IWW organizers were dragged out of bed, manacled, and transported to Duluth by special train. They had all given speeches that were alleged to have incited the Marsonovich boarding house violence. The police there felt it necessary to surround the jail to prevent any attempts by Wobbly sympathizers to rescue "leaders of the gang that has been terrorizing the iron ranges for nearly a month." The *News Tribune* had reported the prisoners being moved for their own safety because a lynching appeared to be brewing.

The Duluth *Weekly Herald* ran a front page story on James C. Myron, "killed last evening in Biwabik by a bullet fired by a striking miner inflamed against law and order by the anarchistic doctrines of the IWW men who are just now making the Range a place where peacefully inclined people cannot reside. . . . Few men in Duluth [were] more popular than Myron."

With several of his organizers already in jail, Haywood sent in Elizabeth Gurley Flynn; a July 12 headline took note of her impending arrival: "Elizabeth Flynn Arrives to Stir Up Strife." Large posters circulated on the streets and appeared in several newspapers, including the New York *Call*, announcing a Declaration of War by the IWW against "the Steel Trust and the independent mining companies of Minnesota" and signed by Big Bill Haywood. On July 14, President Woodrow Wilson took another swipe at foreign-born citizens who "draw apart in spirit and organization to seek some special object of their own. . . . Only true Americans can infect [naturalized citizens] with the spirit of Americanism."

At the preliminary hearing of the thirteen Wobblies charged with killing Myron and Ladvalla, the prosecution claimed those arrested in Virginia (Scarlett, Schmidt, Tresca, Little, and others) had made "inflammatory speeches" that incited the killings. An enthusiastic demonstration with a roar of applause broke out as the defendants entered the courtroom, and Judge W. H. Smallwood repeatedly pounded his gavel to restore order. Scarlett and Schmidt were named as advocates of murder. A witness claimed the latter, speaking on June 15 to a large crowd in Virginia, had said: "If any miner works, even though he is your own brother, go and kill him." Thomas Moodie of Virginia testified that he heard Scarlett instruct strikers to kill three mining company men for every striker, striker's wife, or striker's child killed. The hearing ended with the defendants singing Wobbly songs on the way back to their cells. The majority of those arrested in Virginia, including Frank Little, were released for lack of concrete evidence.

The Duluth *News Tribune* of July 30 included the following report: "Mitchell, SD, vigilantes pledge to rid town of IWW undesirables." This announcement reminds us that the Range is, as Haywood's wire to Tresca said, "a big territory to cover." By extending their net beyond the Range's usual boundaries and into the Dakotas, the Wobblies were seeking to strengthen the miner-harvester united front. This strategy met with stiff resistance from mine owners and farm owners alike.

Immediately following their release from jail, Little, Gilday, Stark, and Russell plunged back into strike work, becoming particularly involved in efforts to support those defendants still incarcerated. To aid this project, Haywood sent in Judge Hilton, who had been Joe Hill's legal counsel, and Leon O. Whitsell, a member of the defense team during the Boise Trial in which Haywood was acquitted of murder. He also deployed seasoned organizer Joe Ettor, himself found innocent of murder during the Lawrence strike, to the Mesabi Range as a fundraiser for the defense. The case was eventually settled through plea bargaining and never came to court, a fact that greatly disgruntled Haywood.

By August 3, Elizabeth Gurley Flynn was working with men she could depend on, Joe Ettor and Frank Little, but her lover, Carlo Tresca, was among those still being held on first-degree murder charges.[3] In all, there were eight seasoned IWW organizers on the Range at that time.

Duluth passed an ordinance prohibiting the IWW from passing out handbills. The union immediately demanded its repeal, and further stated that if the prisoners were not released, the IWW "would close every industry in the United States." In a speech given at Virginia's strike headquarters, Little spoke of his "I don't give a damn" policy as being "the only method to pursue if success for the agitators is to be won." In a story headed, "Little Hits at Authorities/IWW Agitator Brags About Serving Time for Free Speech," he is quoted as telling workers:

> To hell with the governor. . . . The laws of the state and nation are made by men controlled by the Steel Trust. There are only a mere handful of politicians who represent the people and the laws are passed to aid the employers and damage you. It is true there is no law against picketing, but the sheriff in an address tonight declared that more deputies were needed to prevent picketing. . . . I once served 6 months for delivering an address of this nature. . . . Do no act of violence but picket and keep every man from going to work. If a deputy arrests you go peacefully to jail with him. When we get 3000 in jail, the taxpayers will realize, although the sheriff is making a nice little stake by feeding the county prinsoners [sic] at the present time, who followed the red flag of revolution. . . . The sheriff and the governor will begin to squirm when they think of election time in

the near future and they know that they will not be put back in
office. Why they may even have to seek work in the mines.

He concluded with some Wobbly poetry and a plea for "the agitators
facing a life sentence." Governor Burnquist may have done some
squirming, but he was reelected and remained in office until 1921.

Frank Little seems to have felt most at home speaking to workers on the street, or at the scene of their rebellion. He knew the
boxcar circuit, street-level guys who spoke the Wobbly lingo (much
of which is collected in Irving Werstein's *Pie in the Sky: An American
Struggle*). A fellow worker could say to him: "I'm a bindle stiff, a
straw cat, trying to stay south of the bulls. It's all right by me if you
turn the cat loose. I'm no scissor bill or shorthorn either. I can flip
and know a shark when I see one. Sometimes a cat's got to throw
the guts." Frank would listen and know the speaker was a farm laborer, mostly in the hay fields (straw cat), who carried a bed roll
(bindle), and wanted to avoid the police (bulls). It was okay with
him if you committed acts of sabotage (turn the cat loose). He was
class conscious (no scissor bill) and no longer young (no shorthorn). He could hop freight trains (flip) and knew a shady employment agent (shark) when he saw one. Sometimes a hobo (cat) had
to speak his mind (throw the guts).

By mid-August, Little and several other strikers had been deported to Iron River, Michigan. Elizabeth Gurley Flynn recalls traveling with Mary Heaton Vorse to an iron-mining county in
Michigan where "male organizers had been deported. Frank Little
among them." The hobo agitator was arrested on August 16 in Iron
River, abducted from jail and, with a noose round his neck, told to

cease his activities and divulge the names of local leaders. He gave no names, so his assailants knocked him out and left him in a ditch near Watersmeet, Michigan, about thirty-five miles northwest of Iron River.

Considering IWW activities on the Mesabi Range from the vantage point of 1913 as well as 1916 renders one of Frank Little's most significant achievements more clearly visible: uniting the migratory harvester with his counterpart in the mines and the oil fields. He first began organizing oil field workers in Oklahoma in 1912, and then again in 1914 in Drumright, Oklahoma, where his brother Alonzo lived at the time.

So far as the Mesabi conflicts are concerned, Little's blunt statements and relentless determination to hold out against Great Northern Railroad's offers in 1913 would certainly have influenced the steel companies' attitude toward him in 1916. During the earlier conflict, despite the AWO not yet being officially formed, Little informed strikers that harvest work was plentiful and close at hand. This announcement is likely to have further solidified the officials' desire to muzzle him three years later.

The 1913 kidnapping must have left Little with equally ardent supporters and enemies which, consequently, made 1916 more volatile. One wonders if by employing two such "hot blooded" organizers as Tresca and Little, a term he applied to both men, Haywood sought to ignite an already tense situation. But such speculation would be reckless and at odds with certain facts. Despite his allegedly "hot blood" Little had a reputation for nonviolence. He did not endorse Tresca's call for an eye for an eye in the matter of John Alar's murder. Haywood may well have sent him in to ride herd on the more violent predilections of Tresca, Scarlett, and Schmidt. While Little advocated sabotage, he maintained a strict separation between property damage and the loss of profits it caused and violence aimed at human targets. To bundle sabotage with violence under one umbrella is a popular convenience but decidedly unfair to the tactic as it equates damage to property or profit with violence against other human beings. The most frequently used Wobbly sabotage tactic was called "playing the Hoosier," which meant acting like a country bumpkin, playing the fool in response to on-the-job demands, and being clumsy and purposely slow-witted. For the most part destructive methods, like burning crops, were opposed. As Wobbly Jack Miller said, looking back on his past: "If the farmer is disabled, the job stops. We were there to work and earn wages, not to destroy."

The Mesabi Range's largest daily newspaper, the Duluth *News Tribune*, took what can only be described as separate attitudes towards the IWW in general and Frank Little in particular. Comparing those attitudes provides an interesting contrast. From the beginning in 1913, the IWW as an organization is treated with extreme caution. The union seems, at least in part, to have been forever plagued by the WFM's long-standing reputation for violence. Haywood and company being acquitted of the Steunenberg killing did not end talk of WFM violence. Such talk, in jaw-work and ink alike, may well have been accelerated by the verdict.

The IWW we read about in the *News Tribune* is synonymous with trouble of the worst sort. Frank Little, on the other hand, is treated rather well. What is presented of his speeches is reasonable and coherent, informative and potentially instructive. Likewise, the paper covered Little's disappearance with a pronounced lack of skepticism. That only one article appeared on those who thought the whole affair was a propaganda stunt as opposed to four on those who did not question the disappearance's authenticity leans heavily in favor of the believers rather than the scoffers. We find what I would call the *News Tribune*'s strongest feelings against the so-called outside agitator Frank Little in the two cartoons described earlier in this chapter. One is a boot crushing a poisonous snake, the other a boomerang hitting an IWW agitator. The former appeared two days after Little's disappearance while the latter hit the streets the day after Little's description of his ordeal. Appearing when they did, the cartoons illustrate what might be viewed as a developing viewpoint. Killing Little, or "crushing the poisonous snake," was one alternative, but getting him out of the way and seeing what transpired with the strike while he was out of the picture was another. Frank Little's life very likely hung in the balance during those four days on Getty's farm. Without him, the strike broke down. His life was spared. The strike was dead, and he was no longer an important enough figure to warrant further interrogation. One can hardly imagine Haywood or Elizabeth Gurley Flynn being left unquestioned under similar circumstances. In any event, the paper's attitude toward Frank Little demonstrates an unexpected complexity.

Back east, the strike drew some favorable ink from Randolph Bourne. In a *New Republic* piece published three months after the conflict ended, Bourne defended the union's version of what had happened. Interestingly enough, during the 1912–1913 academic year, he had roomed with Harry Chase at Columbia University.

Chase had been the *Daily People*'s business manager and a Wobbly of the political action persuasion who had come to the university, says sociologist Louis Filler, "to prepare himself to serve the Socialist Labor Party more effectively." From Chase, Bourne received an education in IWW theory which, according to Filler, he added to what he'd seen with his "own eyes in Scranton and Gary and Pittsburgh [of] the way workers live, not in crises of industrial labor but in brimming times of peace."

During the period from 1913 to 1916, the two most important events with regard to Little's position in the IWW were his election to the General Executive Board and the success of the Agricultural Workers Organization; the latter of which may have heated up an already brewing tension between a union dominated by its eastern members, run, some might say ruthlessly, by Big Bill Haywood, and a western faction led by Frank Little.

## AGRICULTURAL WORKERS ORGANIZATION (AWO)

Between 1913 and 1916, the emerging AWO pumped new life and money into the IWW and brought the Mesabi Range as well as the surrounding farm country in Minnesota, Wisconsin, and the Dakotas under the union's close scrutiny. Of course harvest work, performed almost entirely by migrant laborers, extended far beyond those four states. In his *Harvest Wobblies*, Greg Hall writes that in Southern California, the Plains states, and the Corn Belt, Wobbly organizers known as job delegates "signed up men in the field while working along with them." The working conditions of these men, women, and children closely resembled those documented by Carleton Parker at Wheatland. Being forced to live on wages from $1.00 to $2.50 for ten-hour workdays kept these laborers constantly on the move looking for their next job. The AWO gave them a strength they had not before known. The union organized strikes for better pay, shorter working hours, and better living conditions. These strikes were usually victorious since the farmer was under pressure exerted by nature to get his crop picked or lose money.

The job delegate system, while defended as the best method of keeping the IWW in the hands of the workers rather than the Chicago leadership, had a tendency to put too much focus on the hobo jungles. The strategy reached more men than on-the-job organizing, but it also resulted in nonunion workers being hired, thereby leaving the IWW with no leverage at the workplace itself. It may well be the jungles' effectiveness as recruiting sites for the free-speech fights that caused organizers, Frank Little among them, to overestimate their value for union organizing.

Little's suggestion at the ninth annual IWW convention in 1914 brought about the formation of a Bureau of Migratory Workers. Its mission was "to set up the conference, coordinate information on jobs, and further organization among harvest workers." In October, *Solidarity* reported that the bureau was working "to combat 'the schemes of labor bureaus and employment sharks' whose exaggerated accounts of labor shortages produced a surplus of labor, driving down wages and forcing many unemployed harvest hands to resort to begging and stealing."

On April 21, 1915, a conference to discuss how best to organize harvesters took place in Kansas City and drew representatives from

Des Moines, Fresno, Minneapolis, Portland, Kansas City, Salt Lake City, and San Francisco. A pal of his, E. F. Doree, a tirelessly active AWO leader, may have been Little's source of insider information at the conference.[4]

After voting against the use of street speaking as a "means of propaganda," the delegates established the Agricultural Workers Organization 400. The new organization's agitation committee put forth a list of demands for the 1915 harvest season, which included "minimum wage of $3.00 for more than ten hours a day; 50 cents overtime for every hour worked above ten in one day; good clean board; good clean places to sleep in, and plenty of clean bedding; and no discrimination against members of the IWW." A notice in the June 26 issue of *Solidarity* informed Kansas and Oklahoma farmers: "The above demands are asked of you, and if granted, satisfactory work will be done." The consequences, should the demands not be met, are left to the reader's imagination.

The Kansas City *Post* ignored the formation of the AWO 400 despite it having occurred in Kansas City. But it did print reports of Kansas farmers "openly proclaiming in alarm that 'they would be at the mercy of the IWW's this summer.'" Those same farmers had dismissed the Wobbly plan as 'wild-eyed,' but turned now in panic to the federal government for help in combating the IWW organizing offensive. In December, 1914, the government had created the National Farm Labor exchange "to recruit workers in anticipation of a labor shortage during wartime." Its Kansas City office played a substantial role in supplying wheat harvesters for Oklahoma, Kansas, Nebraska, and Missouri. According to the IWW, it accomplished this task by recruiting "an oversupply of labor in various grain-growing sections by advertising in large metropolitan dailies in the East." The union also accused the Employment Office of refusing "to send members of the IWW to any job." The Wobblies fought back by keeping their membership secret or renouncing the IWW by tearing up their union cards in front of the bosses. The AWO could easily send them duplicate cards. The objective was to stay on the job so they could continue recruiting and organizing.

The 1915 campaign significantly exceeded IWW expectations. In the period from July 1 to December 31, "the AWO initiated 2,280 members—mostly recruited between June and October—and accumulated $14,113.06 in its treasury. Branches had been established in Des Moines, Kansas City, Salt Lake City, Sioux City, Omaha, Minneapolis, and Duluth" and, according to *Solidarity*, "plans were underway to start one in Sacramento, Calif."

In 1916, as part of an effort to combat the AWO, Midwestern farmers planned on bringing in thirty thousand black harvest hands. The union welcomed this idea, telling "John Farmer" that, according to Philip Foner, "the IWW has some good Negro organizers, just itching for a chance of this kind. Thirty thousand Negroes will come and 30,000 IWW's will go back. The red card is cherished as much and its objects understood as well by a black man as by a white one!" No more was heard of the plan to import black harvesters.

The AWO employed some highly controversial organizing tactics. Frank Little's role in formulating and implementing those tactics is difficult to ascertain. AWO organizers took control of the freight cars used by migratory workers to travel from job to job.

Armed with clubs, pick handles, and guns, they compelled anyone who rode to join the union. Riding without an AWO 400 or IWW card was out of the question. The July 12, 1916, the Emporia *Gazette* complained, "A lawless condition has been created on the freight trains entering North and South Dakota by these men who claim no country and no flag." The AWO claimed only "hijacks, bootleggers, and gamblers" were jettisoned from the trains, but there is notable evidence to the contrary. The *Monthly Labor Review* and *North American Review* carried articles accusing the AWO of offenses "ranging from outright murder to crippling non-cooperative workers by leaving acid in their shoes." The truth of these assertions is hard to assess, but they created a controversy that brought about a split between old time IWW men and the new breed of the AWO 400.

By 1915, Frank Little would certainly have been considered an old-time IWW man, even though he was only thirty-six years old. He may well have believed the 400's methods were too severe. But wouldn't he have had considerable sympathy for the position AWO organizers found themselves in? As early as 1913, before the war in Europe began, newspaper denunciations of the IWW had reached a fever pitch, and the war transformed that fever into hysteria. In such an atmosphere converting workers with nothing but solid, reasonable arguments must have been exceedingly difficult. Their circumstances forced AWO organizers to apply pressure. By keeping those who would not work with the union out of the harvest fields, the AWO was following a well-established policy among industrial unions of keeping scabs out of on-strike factories. Philip S. Foner offers an insightful description of AWO tactics: "In organizing the harvest workers, every freight car, every freight yard, every [hobo] jungle was a picket line. Since the non-cooperative harvesters rode the freight cars, they had to keep off unless they joined up. This was legitimate trade-union procedure, and that it was acknowledged to be such was proven by the fact that the union of railroaders cooperated by asking all free riders for their red membership cards." Foner goes on to say the AWO established a "picket line over a thousand miles, from the harvest fields of Northern Oklahoma to the northern wheat fields of Canada."

While Little's public oratory remained strictly nonviolent, one cannot help wondering if the storming of a Letcher, South Dakota, jail by three hundred harvest workers, the majority of whom were AWO/Wobblies, in order to free two of their fellow workers incarcerated for disorderly conduct, did not bring a smile to his face. After all, the jail-filling, budget-busting strategy of the free-speech actions had run its course. Little's always-on-strike credo and the political climate mandated action of a more aggressive sort.

According to the AWO, its 1916 campaign recruited nearly sixteen thousand members. IWW income at the end of that fiscal year was $49,114.84, an increase of approximately 300 percent over the previous year. In evaluating these figures we must bear in mind that the increased membership included seasonal workers from other industries as well as agricultural, thereby giving the AWO a rapidly growing, united-front authority and further developing the IWW vision of forming "One Big Union." Proof of the AWO's rising power may best be seen in Bill Haywood's jealousy of it. According to Nigel Sellars, in March 1917, Big Bill and his supporters on the GEB "stripped the organization of its nonagricultural workers." While oil workers remained "technically" under the AWO umbrella, the headquarters in Chicago took charge of the other branches. The union was also renamed Agricultural Workers Industrial Union (AWIU) no. 400. Bill Haywood's actions provide further evidence of his growing fear of Frank Little's influence and power.


## OIL WORKERS INDUSTRIAL UNION (OWIU)

Thanks to Nigel Sellars, our first confirmed sighting of Frank Little organizing oil workers occurs, not surprisingly, in Oklahoma. As pointed out in the last chapter, Little became ill during the 1911 Kansas City free-speech action. He left there in December and traveled to Guthrie to stay with Mrs. Allie L. Cox until he recovered. From there he reported to *Solidarity* on conditions in his home state. By January 1912, he was attempting to revive the Oklahoma City local and organize an oil workers local in Drumright. But his efforts were not successful. According to Sellars, by 1913 no IWW locals existed in Oklahoma. In 1914, Tulsa had fifteen thousand men, nearly half the city's total population, "looking for oil field work," victims of a "huge labor surplus." "Illegal alcohol, prostitution, and gambling" were rampant. Oil boomtowns, like western mining towns, had "a huge influx of generally itinerant people, poor quality housing, and lots of easy money." Naturally, vice was on the scene in as many forms as the market could bear. Wobblies as individuals issued reports on working conditions in Oklahoma, but the union had no organized presence until, as Sellars puts it, "an emerging oil boom and the state and federal government's botched attempt to control the wheat harvest job market gave the IWW renewed life."

Little's initial lack of success in organizing oil workers was perhaps to be expected when one considers the situation more closely. The workers fit into three rough-and-ready categories. First came the "boomers"—oil riggers, drillers, toil-dressers, storage-tank builders, and such—who created the work site. Paid well at six or seven dollars for a twelve-hour workday, they were usually young and single; the company believed unmarried men were more pliable than their married counterparts. Next, we have the unskilled "boll weevils"—farm laborers who worked the oil sites to make ends meet during hard times for agriculture. Last, and perhaps valued least, were the "drifters"—older, often alcohol- or drug-addicted men, sometimes ex-convicts, of dubious reliability.

Three factors made oil workers more difficult to organize than harvest hoboes. First, the better-paid boomers, often employed by outside contractors, saw no need for a union. The boll weevils, also known as "roustabouts," generally shared this view, since they were often married men from rural areas who planned on returning to the farm when the job was finished. Second, a strict hierarchy was maintained among the workers; boomers had nothing to do with boll weevils and drifters. Nigel Sellars writes that fiercely anti-union oil companies intensified the class divisions imposed by the workers themselves by setting "the few black and Mexican workers against the whites to keep wages low." In addition, boom-town businessmen demonstrated a fondness for forming Ku Klux Klan chapters. Third, the nomadic lifestyle of migratory workers meant they were often at another job before a workplace complaint could be resolved.

In late 1913, the GEB sent organizers into Tulsa and Drumright; in the latter city Little and A. W. Rockwell eventually organized a local. Tulsa authorities' fear of the IWW caused them to
pass ordinances prohibiting street meetings. As we have seen before, this tactic was routinely employed against the union. The
Wobbly contention that their ability to function effectively hinged
on their right to hold such meetings seems unassailable.

Frank Little, Ethel Carpenter, and E. J. Foote encouraged a
policy that embraced the migratory workers; a pragmatic decision
as the union had been more successful with migratory than settled
workers, especially in the West. In 1914, Sellars tells us "the boom
towns and wheat fields of Oklahoma served as testing grounds," recruiting sites for those migrant workers "the IWW then believed
were the vanguard of the revolution."

Cushing oil worker James Keon thought the IWW ideology
was tailor made for Oklahoma oil fields, and in 1916 wrote Bill Haywood asking him to institute an aggressive organizing campaign in
"the Midcontinent oil fields of Northern Texas, Oklahoma, and
southern Kansas." The potential for strengthening the united front,
to which Frank Little had clearly dedicated himself, was considerable as an increasing number of harvest hands worked as pipeliners
and ditchers during the fall and winter. The founding of the Oil
Workers Industrial Union (OWIU) frightened business executives
and government officials. The companies had more problems than
just labor unrest, of which there was plenty; charges of war profi-
teering had also been leveled against them. What better time to
claim that the IWW posed a direct threat to the war effort? The organizing of oil workers the IWW and Frank Little helped initiate

opened up new frontiers for the labor movement at a crucial time in American history. Oil was certainly a wartime necessity, and Oklahoma was the country's largest producer of petroleum, just as the Mesabi Range in Northern Minnesota was the nation's largest source of another wartime necessity—iron ore. The IWW's opponent in Minnesota was Andrew Carnegie and the Steel Trust, while in Oklahoma the union faced John D. Rockefeller and Standard Oil. In placing the blame for the assassination of Frank Little neither of these economic-political powers should be excluded from consideration.

# CHAPTER FOUR
# Urgency and Conspiracy

## FRANK LITTLE'S LAST YEAR

As the once-radical Western Federation of Miners became increasingly more conservative, culminating in its decision to join the American Federation of Labor, tensions between the WFM and IWW mounted. The dynamiting of the WFM union hall in Butte on June 13, 1914, brought the conflict between the two unions to a head. Paul Frederick Brissenden's description of the WFM-IWW split reminds us that the friction between the two unions, while certainly an element in "the dynamiting outrage," had become quite intense. He describes two factions, radical "Reds" and conservative "Yellows;" the latter "comprised the local officials of the union and their followers." Among the former "IWW members and sympathizers predominated." The Reds claimed union leadership "packed the hall with reactionaries before the [official] hour of opening, so that the 'Reds' could not even voice their grievances."

In a June 29, 1914, letter to the *Denver United Labor Bulletin*, Lewis J. Duncan, Butte's socialist mayor, claimed "the responsibility for Tuesday's disturbance cannot truthfully be placed on the I.W.W. The 600 itinerant I.W.W. troublemakers on whom your report lays the blame for the June 13th trouble are non-existent." Duncan goes on to identify the rebels against WFM officials as "a majority of the miners of Butte, and only a small minority of them . . . are even sympathetic with the I.W.W.s." By contrast "scarcely more than a week after the dynamiting" the local press reported an assembly of five thousand miners, men called "seceders" from the WFM who had formed "an executive committee of twenty, a majority of whom are known to be members of the Industrial Workers of the World." Such may have been the case, but not until 1916 was there an official IWW local in Butte. At the 1916 WFM convention, Haywood's former co-defendant Charles H. Moyer, president of the WFM, blamed the Butte bombing on a "'poison I.W.W. promoters were scattering' in the minds of Butte miners." In the summer of 1917, Frank Little was murdered—or, to be more precise, assassinated.

The last year of the hobo agitator's life revolves around three primary actions: first, a copper miners' strike in Arizona and subsequent deportation of miners; second, resisting the draft and organizing a general strike in protest against US involvement in the European war; third, a strike by Butte miners, during the course of which Frank Little was assassinated.

By 1917, Little was chairman of the General Executive Board of the IWW. Ralph Chaplin remembers Frank introducing him to officers of the various industrial unions.

Gene Lantz informs us that on July 2, 1917, Little advised Bisbee, Arizona, miners not to strike. Then, not a week later, Little broke his ankle "in a car wreck in Bisbee." Elizabeth Gurley Flynn and others support the car wreck story, but say nothing else about the hobo agitator's activities in Bisbee. While Lantz's report on Little's advice to the workers appears to contradict one of the hobo agitator's long-held principles, we should not forget he voiced his always-on-strike policy in 1913, the year before war broke out in Europe. By 1916, Little may have come around to Haywood's more cautious stance against striking while US soldiers were being killed in Europe. Taking a more moderate line on strikes would not have interfered with Little's opposition to the draft. However, advising against a specific strike might have significantly diminished the spirit of resistance needed for a general strike. This is almost certainly one of the most urgent and difficult decisions Little faced during the last months of his life. His broken ankle saved him from being deported with the others at Bisbee. After the car accident, Little organized from a bunk in a miner's home.

Quite early on the morning of July 10, 1917, ten armed agents of the United Verde Copper company in Jerome, Arizona, rousted miners from their homes and the most militant seventy of these suspected rebels were loaded into cattle cars and delivered to California. Two days later, in Bisbee, 1,162 miners were pulled out of bed and marched to a baseball park, close by the train station, before being shipped in freight and cattle cars to Hermanas Desert and left without food or water. When Bill Haywood received the news, he imme-diately telegraphed Woodrow Wilson "demanding that the miners be returned to their homes, and there be protected from the fury of the mob." Wilson made no reply. Haywood amongst others thought the actions carried out against the miners were ordered by business inter-ests, particularly the copper trust. Those interests called themselves "The Vigilante Committee." The American Protective League, spon-sored by the US Department of Justice, may have also had a hand in the deportations. Similar deportations during the 1916 Mesabi iron miners' strike foreshadow the Jerome and Bisbee incidents, as the lat-ter foreshadow the Palmer raids.

Haywood was told the abducted miners had been transported to Columbus, New Mexico. He wired President Wilson a second time but again received no answer. In Haywood's opinion, the Bis-bee incident fueled the flames of those agitating for a general strike he opposed. As the IWW's most fiery opponent to US involve-ment in the war, Frank Little spearheaded the movement for a gen-eral strike.

On or about July 17, Arnon Gutfeld reports that Little "boasted" to the *Butte Miner* about having made the following re-marks to the governor of Arizona Campbell: "Governor, I don't give a damn what country your country is fighting, I am fighting for the solidarity of labor."

Besides the war and conscription, the IWW was facing some tough choices, and vital issues concerning the AWO were coming to a head. If the union allowed tenant farmers and sharecroppers to join, those new members would have been employers—and po-tential exploiters—of at least some of the farm laborers who were already IWW-AWO members. But, by excluding tenant farmers and sharecroppers the IWW was turning its back on thousands of new members. In 1914, Wobbly leadership had excluded them and, according to historian Covington Hall, made one of its "biggest mistakes"; consequently, the Working Class Union was formed. In his master's thesis on the Green Corn Rebellion, Charles C. Bush sternly says of that union: "The Working Class Union was the direct result of the prevailing spirit of discontent and the tendency to organize every passing whim into some form of society."

One wonders where Frank Little stood on the exclusion question. His colleague Ethel Carpenter characterized the farmers as "capitalists at heart, no different from other employers." In a *Solidarity* piece entitled "Keep Out the Farmer," William Mead compares farmers to lawyers, saying they are both parasites who must take a "back seat for the good and welfare of our movement." But, according to Nigel Sellars, Little's confidant E. F. Doree believed it was wrong to treat tenants like capitalists. As an organizer, Little would certainly have been alive to the tension allowing them to join the union would have caused. Tenant farmers and sharecroppers found themselves in a no man's land of sorts, so far as the class war was concerned. They were men with capitalist dreams but little else. Their economic independence, as such, was increasingly on the wane as they were increasingly forced to become farm laborers, which meant being paid subsistence wages. After being denied IWW membership, these disappointed farmers, many of whom had undoubtedly heard Frank Little speak at various socialist clubs, went on to become members of the WCU.

The WCU was socialist and decentralized in the best western Wobbly sense. Each local had its own tenets. According to Charles C. Bush, the WCU leadership had not separated itself entirely from the IWW. He tells his readers that J. E. Wiggins, the alleged head of the WCU, "advocated extreme syndicalism and open revolution." Bush further contends that Wiggins was an "I.W.W. agitator" who had done a lot of jail time in the Northwest. But the image originally presented to the public by the WCU, while socialist, was not revolutionary. It wanted nothing more than the "improvement of its members' economic conditions," though its social function was of no small importance. It allowed members "to exchange opinions, listen to the advice of more successful neighbors, and enjoy a little fraternal association." As the western Wobbly union halls had educated its members in radical ideas, WCU halls guided its members toward the objective of succeeding within the system. Where does so revolutionary a figure as J. E. Wiggins fit into the WCU's public objectives? To a syndicalist revolutionary the union's objectives would be of little use other than as a front for more subversive activity. "Claiming the WCU was simply the IWW by another name," writes Nigel Sellars, "Oklahoma newspapers began a jingoistic campaign against the Wobblies. Some editors openly called for lynch mobs to deal with those whom one United States senator styled 'Imperial Wilhelm's Warriors.'"

We have seen how America's entry into World War One unsettled Bill Haywood, leaving him unable to take a consistent stance on whether or not workers should register for the draft. But for the Canadian Valley tenant farmers of eastern Oklahoma a stance was simple: They did not want to go to war, and they did not want their boys to go. They preferred to be left alone. According to Charles C. Bush, Haywood sent in organizer H. H. "Rube" Munson "to reorganize the WCU along more radical lines." Munson was allegedly the object of an intensive search by Chicago police and, therefore, happy to take the assignment. Bush writes: "He was a professional, and he knew the tricks of the trade." Munson quickly chose three men to serve as assistants: Roy Crane, an unstable "chronic disturber," Homer Spence, a farmer from near Tate, Oklahoma, who "assumed an active, although none too courageous leadership," and W. L. Benefield who "became a local 'captain' and an advocate of the most extreme measures." A portion of the WCU membership thought of the United States as "Rockefeller's country" while others thought it belonged to J. P. Morgan. But for our purposes these are secondary concerns; more to the point is the size and militancy of the Green Corn Rebellion's resistance to the draft.

With the entry of the United States into the war, a full-scale antimilitary, antidraft campaign began in Oklahoma. Approximately thirty-five thousand poorly educated, poverty-stricken tenant farmers and sharecroppers had not been converted by a widespread and relatively sophisticated pro-war propaganda campaign. Instead, Bush tells us, they "accepted the weird tales of an unknown Chicago criminal [Munson] as the whole truth." Nigel Sellars refutes the idea held by "writers both sympathetic to and hostile to the WCU" that Henry H. "Rube" Munson was fleeing a "criminal indictment" and had been sent to Oklahoma by the IWW leadership. Sellars writes: "Munson was a former lead and zinc miner from the tri-state town of Seneca, Missouri, where his family lived with his wife's parents.

He had organized for the WCU for two years by 1917. It is highly un-likely that Munson was a Wobbly as the IWW had virtually no pres-ence in the Tri-State region until the early 1920s." Munson was charged in the massive federal indictment late in 1917 "along with more than 160 others—many of them non-Wobblies."

We know the Oklahoma tenant farmers and sharecroppers were far from alone in opposing conscription, which is useful in helping to explain why newspaper accounts of the draft resisters consistently describe them as cowards who, despite vastly superior numbers, nearly always ran when confronted by a lawman and his posse. Cowardice has long been the easiest and most convenient way of explaining draft resistance. Munson's exaggerated prophe-cies may have set the resisters' fighting spirit up for a fall. He and his three officers told their followers the rebellion would be over four million strong. It was, in fact, nowhere near that size. Munson likewise promised the rebels superior numbers to the US military, as the latter was busy with the war in Europe.

At about four o'clock in the afternoon on August 2, the day after Frank Little was murdered, the Green Corn Rebellion began when Sheriff Frank Grall and his deputy, J. W. Cross, were am-bushed. Deputy Cross caught a bullet in the throat, while the sher-iff's horse was brought down under him. The rebellion had originally been scheduled to start promptly at midnight, Friday, August 3, and was to be simultaneous throughout the area. Did the news of Frank Little's murder cause the uprising to begin nearly a full day early? (Another question: Were the forest fires in the Northwest, said to have been started by the IWW, another act of retaliation for the lynching?) Oklahoma was, after all, Little's home state. Moreover, he was chairman of the union's General Executive Board and a widely known fellow worker; the latter is clearly attested to by the federal government naming the hobo agitator as a co-conspirator with more than one hundred sixty fellow workers.

Nigel Sellars describes the action against Sheriff Grall and his deputy as well as the events shortly thereafter: "Within hours raiding parties had cut telegraph and telephone lines, burned railroad bridges, and allegedly dynamited pipelines near Healdton." He goes on to say, "The IWW took no part in the Green Corn Rebellion and had only a slender indirect connection to the Working Class Union." Sellars feels the tenant farmers put IWW ideology to their own purposes. He remarks that the "evangelical, millenarian style of its rhetoric" made the IWW brand of syndicalism awfully appealing to tenant farmers. Ideologically, the great bulk of the WCU appears to have been socialist-populist, at least officially, but the press and authorities repeatedly spoke of it, as they did the IWW, as a gang of anarchists. The Oklahoma press' portrayal of the rebellion has an almost cartoon-like quality. The rebels are simple-minded, gutless anarchists while lawmen are invariably bold and brave. Charles C. Bush thoroughly documents the local newspapers' oftentimes wildly divergent reportage of events.

◆

On June 8, 1917, a fire occurred at the Speculator Mine in Butte, which killed 164 men. Anaconda Copper Company controlled, but apparently did not own, the Speculator Mine. The company was charged with neglecting safety regulations. Manholes that should have provided escape paths for miners did not conform to the standards specified by law. Nearly half the victims were burned beyond recognition.

Intense and long-brewing tensions were coming to a head in the Pacific Northwest by the summer of 1917. Butte was the center of the number one copper-producing district in the world, and for a period of fourteen years—from 1889 to 1903—the city was known as the Gibraltar of Unionism. Those years were the golden era of labor in Butte because, as Arnon Gutfeld writes, "The War of the Copper Kings had been fought in the political arena, labor's votes and support had become objects to be courted and bought. After 1903, the situation changed radically as labor engaged in internecine warfare and was faced with the powerful united mine owners." Gutfeld goes on to say the IWW attempted to fill the void created by labor's lost power. He also accuses the IWW of having used the unskilled migratory workers it organized "sometimes cruelly and cynically," but fails to offer any support for his claim.

From 1912 to 1917, the Company—as Montana residents called the Anaconda Copper Mining Company—rode firmly in the saddle and labor was its horse. Once a closed shop, Butte became an open shop. "Rustling cards," issued by the Company, were required of all prospective workers, and said cards were not issued to those deemed troublemakers. Collective bargaining ended, and individual bargaining ensued. Riots were not uncommon, and militia too often patrolled Butte's streets. The Speculator Mine fire was the proverbial straw that broke the camel's back. Five days after the fire, on June 13, 1917, the Metal Mine Workers Union (MMWU) was established. The new union made seven demands: first, recognition of the union as the miners' bargaining agent; second, abolition of the rustling card; third, no more blacklisting; fourth, discharge of Montana's mining inspector; fifth, strict enforcement of state mining laws; sixth, higher wages; and seventh, right of free speech and assemblage.

The Company's response appeared on the front page of the Butte *Daily Post*—a paper owned by Anaconda Copper. (In 1917 Anaconda owned two newspapers, the *Daily Post* and the *Anaconda Standard*. Within a few years, the Company owned four more of the state's seven major papers. Gutfeld notes, "The weekly newspapers in Montana stuck close to the company line, for they depended on county printing contracts.") The *Daily Post* blamed the IWW for Butte's problems and claimed Butte miners were "the highest paid in the world." In any case, the paper said the IWW was leading the strike and the company would not negotiate with Wobblies. By June 29, fifteen thousand men, including the Metal Trades, Machinists, Boilermakers, and Blacksmiths, were on strike. Production was at a virtual standstill. The Company-controlled press accused the IWW of being in league with Germany and thereby treasonous. Senator Charles Thomas of Colorado alleged that the copper strikes were being paid for with "German gold." There were, as economist Philip Taft points out, also "widespread reports of an IWW plot to burn the crops in the Middle West grain belt," but "no source was given for the stories, nor was any proof of the existence of a plan to destroy the grain areas presented." Arizona senator Henry Ashurst claimed IWW stood for "Imperial Wilhelm's Warriors."

The tensions in the Pacific Northwest were not confined to copper miners. Labor conditions in the area demanded action and, as Philip Taft reports, "by the summer of 1917 the Spokane District of the lumber industry was, according to one of its leading organizers, about 70 percent organized in the I.W.W." The Lumber Workers' Industrial Union No. 500, called a strike for July 1, 1917, though the IWW can hardly be said to have initiated the strike as large numbers of workers left their jobs a good two weeks before the stop-work day announced by the Wobblies. In mid-June, lumber workers near Sand Point, Idaho, left their posts and, as Robert Tyler writes, "The sudden strike, like a spark to a string of firecrackers, set off similar protests all over the Pacific Northwest." Tyler believes two things allowed the IWW to "grab the reins of a runaway strike." First, "Wobbly 'delegates' were frequently the natural leaders in the camps," and second, "for better or worse, the I.W.W. was the only instrument available." Within a short time, all the logging east of the Cascade Range had stopped. Tyler tells us the Wobblies and a newly founded AFL union called The International Union of Timber Workers, "co-belligerents if not actual allies, closed down 90 percent of the logging and milling operations in western Washington."

Tyler tells us Washington governor Ernest Lister supported the strikers' "legitimate" demands while at the same time "forcibly suppressing the I.W.W." He publicly supported the eight-hour day, urging employers to incorporate it into their policies. Lister also "defended the I.W.W." when he told a Methodist conference only 10 percent of the Wobblies were 'bad men.'" But the governor's pronouncements ring rather hollow when we discover Lister had earlier "proposed a state-wide organization of vigilantes, a 'Patriotic

League,' with branches in every county." Men were detained on the street and searched for the red cards that would show them to be Wobblies. Checks were also administered on "regularly scheduled passenger trains in the state, like Military Police during war looking for soldiers A.W.O.L." The Oregon National Guard stationed in Washington during the crisis raided an IWW hall in North Yakima and held thirty men "incommunicado" while federal authorities grilled them for possible infractions of the Espionage Act or draft evasion. "Governor Moses Alexander of Idaho toured his state," writes Tyler, "making patriotic appeals to the striker, and cooperating with federal authorities in arresting Wobblies and putting them in stockades and 'bull pens'—familiar and almost institutionalized features of labor unrest in Idaho."

In mid-July, the Company dealt the striking Butte miners a serious blow by offering new contracts to the trade unions. Worker solidarity did not prevail, and the contracts were accepted. A few miners went back to work, but the issues that originally caused them to strike had not been resolved. Frank Little arrived in Butte on July 18, and the following day spoke to a crowd of six thousand men at the city's baseball park. The Butte *Miner* described Little as "a frail man supporting the weight of his body with the aid of crutches, his face contorted with physical pain and the passion which rocked his body, the speaker worked himself into a maniacal fury as he denounced the capitalists of every class and nationality."

The press's response to the speech was shrill, outraged, frightened. An editorial published in the *Daily Missoulian* on July 22 quoted liberally from Little's remarks, ending with "a call for swift action against Little by federal authorities." He had made powerful enemies in Missoula at least as far back as the free-speech struggle of 1909.

Anaconda's chief counsel, L. O. Evans, admitted the company used detectives to infiltrate MMWU and IWW meetings. According to Gutfeld, "Little was the only [IWW] organizer allowed to attend and to speak at the closed meetings of the M.M.W.U." A North Butte Company spy, Carl Dilling, reported Little wanting "the union to fight the companies and to force those miners who had returned [to work] to walk out again." Anaconda detective Warren D. Bennett reported likewise. An anonymous spy describing a July 25 closed IWW meeting at Finnlander Hall attributes the following comments to Frank Little: "We have no set rules to go by, but we organized [sic], call a strike, and use any means necessary to win that strike, and that is the reason the boss don't like us, he can't handle us, and he knows that we will handle him in the near future. . . . Use any means necessary, it don't make any difference what those 'means' are, but use them to win your strike." According to the same anonymous informant on July 26, Little scolded MMWU leaders for their lack of militancy, saying: "You fellows are conducting a peaceful strike. Great God! What would Uncle Sam say to the Soldiers he is sending to meet the German Army if they *laid down their arms* and said *we* are conducting a peaceful war."

On July 23, Frank Little wrote Bill Haywood a letter urging him to make a statement to the public against the war. He received the following reply, dated July 27: "After the statement in this week's *Solidarity* by the Editor it would be superfluous to publish the statement of the Board, as it is practically the same and covers the same essential points." Taft informs us that the GEB's statement, "which was never adopted (it was in the files and seized by the government), denounced wars and reiterated the organization's opposition to them. It warned against suppression of free speech under the 'cloak of military expediency' and argued that as the IWW always opposed war its members were just as entitled to exemption from military service as the Quakers and other religious sects."

Little gave his second public speech in Butte on July 27 during which, according to the Butte *Daily Post*, he said the US Constitution is a "mere scrap of paper which can be torn up" and called President Woodrow Wilson a "lying tyrant." The *Daily Post* judged the talk a "treasonable tirade" and asked the town, "How Long Is It Going to Stand for the Seditious Talk of the I.W.W. Agitator?" District attorney Burton K. Wheeler wanted to prosecute the hobo agitator under the Espionage Act of 1917, but L. O. Evans "was unable to point out any explicit provisions under which Little could be charged." According to Gutfeld, "several labor leaders believed that Little's speeches injured the cause of labor." William F. Dunne, editor of the Butte *Bulletin*, seemed convinced "those in the I.W.W. [who] were agents of the companies" had orchestrated Little coming to Butte.

On August 1, Frank Little was assassinated. The following day's edition of the *Anaconda Standard* quoted deputy US attorney James Baldwin as saying Little's death "was not a case of lynching by a mob, but a case of cold-blooded and premeditated murder." District attorney Wheeler wired the attorney general saying that he had received a report Little's killers were wearing army uniforms. Montana congresswoman Jeannette Rankin stated on the floor of Congress that she had been warned about the impending murder but had not had time to tell the president or any of his cabinet.

The August 2 Butte *Bulletin* claimed it had "sufficient evidence to indicate the names of five men ["William Oates, Herman Gillies, Pete Beadin, a rat named Middleton and . . . a chief gunman named Ryan"] who took part [in the killing], everyone of whom is a company stool pigeon." The paper went on to note, "every man, woman, and child in the country knows that Company agents perpetrated this foulest of all crimes." The *Bulletin's* "sufficient evidence" was never revealed, and a coroner's jury found Frank Little to have been "killed by persons unknown."

On August 5, Frank Little's funeral was the largest ever held in Montana. At least three thousand people marched in the four-mile procession from Duggan Funeral Home to Mountain View Cemetery while thousands more watched. A red silk banner inscribed "a martyr to solidarity" covered the casket. The burial did not include a religious ceremony. "La Marseillaise" was sung as the hobo agitator's remains were lowered into the ground. On August 10, federal troops were deployed to Butte and remained there until long after the war ended.[1]

Less than two weeks after Little's murder, the governors of Montana, Utah, Washington, Oregon, Idaho, and Nevada met at Portland, Oregon, to discuss, as Tyler tells us, "the I.W.W. menace in the West. Governor Sam Stewart of Montana was selected to see President Wilson and to convince him to take action against the Wobblies." On August 13, an anti-sedition bill was put forth by Montana Senator Myers, who claimed he did so because of Little's murder. After being shelved by the US Senate, Myers's bill became the Montana Sedition Act and was eventually incorporated into the Federal Sedition Act of 1918. The assassination of Frank

Little played a central, perhaps even pivotal, role in the campaign to crush the IWW in the Pacific Northwest; which, as Robert Tyler informs us, culminated with a declaration of martial law in Spokane on August 19, the closing of that city's IWW hall, and the arrest of twenty-seven Wobblies. According to Tyler, "The wounded I.W.W. that survived the years from 1917 to 1920 seemed to lose all of its old dash, all of its genius for improvising guerilla tactics."

The national press reaction to Frank Little being killed was, given the circumstances, pretty much what one might expect. According to Carl H. Chrislock, author of *Watchdog of Liberty*, the August 4 issue of the *New York Times* called the lynching "'deplorable and detestable,' but then softened the impact of this judgment by charging that the IWW agitators are in effect, perhaps in fact, agents of Germany." The *Times* said, "Federal authorities should make short work of these treasonable conspirators against the United States." This charge was frequently made, but no concrete evidence linking the IWW to Germany has ever been produced.

The socialist *New York Call* ran the following lead for a piece on August 2: "Organizer for the I.W.W. hung from trestle by masked murderers." From *Solidarity*, on August 11, came an editorial cartoon portraying the Copper Trust, in the shadow of Frank Little's hanging corpse, giving money to the press and saying: "It's alright, pal; just tell them he was a traitor." The public had been well primed to believe Little was a traitor and in large part accepted the idea without question. That he had been a royal pain in the neck to the Copper Trust since 1903 was by no means common knowledge. Though Little was a formidable adversary, the war and a well-orchestrated anti-Wobbly hysteria offered the Copper Trust a perfect opportunity to eliminate him.

On August 25 *Solidarity* published the poem "To Frank Little," written by Viola Gilbert Snell.

Traitor and demagogue,
Wanton breeder of discontent—
That is what they called you—
Those cowards, who condemn sabotage
But hide themselves
Not only behind masks and cloaks
But behind all the armored positions.
Of property and prejudice and the law.
Staunch friend and comrade,
Soldier of solidarity—
Like some bitter magic
The tale of your tragic death
Has spread throughout the land,
And from a thousand miles
Has torn the last shreds of doubt
Concerning might and right.
Young and virile and strong—
Like grim sentinels they stand
Awaiting every opportunity
To break another
Of slavery's chains.
For whatever stroke is needed.
They are preparing.
So shall you be avenged.

The September 2 issue of *Solidarity* featured "Hanged at Midnight," which is the opening section of the poem, an excerpt of which is presented below.

## WHEN THE COCK CROWS

To the Memory of Frank Little

Hanged at Midnight

By Arturo Giovannitti

I

SIX MEN drove up to his house at midnight, and
  woke the poor woman who kept it,
And asked her: "Where is the man who spoke
  against war and insulted the Army?"
And the old woman took fear of the men and the hour, and
  showed them the room where he slept,
And when they made sure it was he whom they
  wanted, they dragged him out of his bed with
  blows, tho' he was willing to walk,
And they fastened his hands on his back, and they
  drove him across the black night,
And there was no moon and no stars and not any
  visible thing, and even the faces of the men
were eaten with the leprosy of the dark, for they
  were masked with black shame.
And nothing showed in the gloom save the glow of
  his eyes and the flame of his soul that scorched
  the face of Death.

II

NO ONE gave witness of what they did to him, after
  they took him away, until a dog barked at his
  corpse.
But I know, for I have seen masked men with the
  rope, and the eyeless things that howl against
  the sun, and I have ridden beside the hangman
  at midnight.
They kicked him, they cursed him, they pushed
  him, they spat on his cheeks and his brow.
They stabbed his ears with foul oaths, they
  smeared his clean face with the pus of their
  ulcerous words.
And nobody saw or heard them. But I call you to
  Witness, John Brown, I call you to witness, you
  Molly Maguires,
And you, Albert Parsons, George Engle, Adolph
  Fischer, August Spies,
And you, Leo Frank, kinsman of Jesus, and you,
  Joe Hill, twice my germane in the rage of the
  song and the fray.
And all of you, sun-dark brothers, and all of you
  harriers of torpid paths, hasteners of the great
  day, propitiators of the holy deed.
I call you all to the bar of the dawn to give witness
  if this is not what they do in America when
  they wake up men at midnight to hang them
  until they're dead.[2]

# ONE HUNDRED AND SIXTY-SIX
# CO-CONSPIRATORS

Liam Donovan did not like to argue, but his pal Jack Fitzgibbons enjoyed nothing more. Jack said, "I tell you it's all show. That bunch isn't a lick different than any of the other rat meat we got locked up here." Jack knew what those Wobblies were up to and was not buying any talk about them being victims of some sort, much less heroes. As far as he could see the ones that weren't Reds were slackers and whiners, and he had no use for any of them.

"Maybe so," Liam replied, avoiding his friend's eager gaze by looking at the floor, "but if I ever heard sincerer words come out of anybody's mouth I don't remember when."

Liam and Jack were guards at the Cook County Jail and on duty when the first batch of Wobblies were booked. They heard the following exchange:

Guard: "What is your religion?"

Prisoner: "The Industrial Workers of the World."

Guard: "That's no religion."

Prisoner: "It's the only one I've got."

Jack raised his voice: "Slimy bastards got a lot of nerve bringing religion into it."

"Maybe that's how they really feel."

"Hell, Liam, everybody knows Reds don't have feelings or religion neither."

Liam let the matter drop. Maybe Jack was right. He sounded awfully sure of himself. But those same Wobblies staged 'entertainments' with hand-held programs included, announcing calisthenics led by William Turner, a Finnish Wobbly, anecdotes and fables with Bill Haywood and sing-alongs. Liam had to smile, for he knew Jack could not deny that those events were unprecedented.

◆

On September 5, 1917, federal agents simultaneously raided forty-six Wobbly offices and the national headquarters in Chicago, confiscating tons of IWW documents. Bill Haywood knew President Woodrow Wilson had appointed Judge J. Harry Covington of the District of Columbia Supreme Court to head a special committee to investigate the union and offered to make IWW files available for Covington and his committee's inspection. But the judge ignored the offer. Apparently, the government preferred to stage well-publicized raids.

While *Solidarity* editor Ralph Chaplin was putting the paper's latest edition to bed, his wife, Edith, asked federal agents for a search warrant to enter the Chaplins' apartment. The agents replied, "What's wrong with you, lady? You're lucky we didn't break down your door. We got the right, you know." At the union's national headquarters, Haywood and his staff valiantly tried to perform their normal duties amid more than two dozen government agents frantically searching for incriminating evidence. Suddenly one of the agents cried out, "What in God's name is this?" His colleagues converged on the agent who had in his hands a plaster cast—ghastly white, its eyes shut and mouth twisted in agony.

Haywood replied, "It's the death mask of a metal miner murdered in Butte, Montana." Thus was Frank Little present on that day—exactly a month after his funeral. He surfaced again when Ralph Chaplin's seven-year-old son, Vonnie, was turned over to two federal agents by his decidedly nervous teacher. The agents offered the boy a ride home, and he replied: "I'll walk." One of the agents grinned at the lad and asked, "Now why would you rather walk than ride?"

"Because I know what happened to Frank Little when he went riding with fellows like you," the boy answered.

On September 28, 1917, 165 alleged IWW members (Nigel Sellars believes many of them were not in fact Wobblies) were indicted on four counts of criminal conspiracy. The indictment said they had conspired with Frank Little, and diverse other persons unknown, by force to prevent, hinder, and delay the execution of eleven different acts of Congress and Presidential Proclamations providing for the execution of the war. They were also accused of interfering with the execution of certain contracts, conspiracy to encourage refusal to the military draft (the Supreme Court had ruled that opposition to the draft was punishable as a "clear and present danger"), conspiracy to cause insubordination in the armed services, and conspiracy to defraud employers hiring certain workers. Many of the accused surrendered the day after the indictment was issued. By the end of 1917, one hundred and twenty of them, following the advice of the IWW's chief counsel, George F. Vanderveer, had turned themselves in and were either incarcerated or on bond.

Ralph Chaplin recalled leaving the federal courthouse with his fellow prisoners, en route to Cook County Jail, and seeing the marquee of a third-rate movie house across the street reading, "The Menace of the I.W.W." and in big red letters "THE RED VIPER."

The prisoners were initially housed in a second galley tier of two-man cells. Chaplin was paired with George Andreytchine, who expressed a particular displeasure for the jazz he could hear coming from a Clark Street nightclub.

The lights suddenly blazing over the catwalk were accompanied by a cry of "cups out!" as a new day began in Cook County Jail. Each cell received two cups of coffee and tin plates of corn grits. Chaplin speaks of the jail as "a monstrous cage" filled with "unearthly nightmarish birds." But then he was not so accustomed to jailhouse life as those who had been in and out of "stir" several times. They did not hear the noise "fresh fish" like Chaplin complained of. Only occasionally when the moon was full did the boys who lived "life on the installment plan" feel any of the frenzy that haunted Ralph Chaplin.

The Wobblies were moved to a cell block once occupied by the Haymarket Five, who had been sentenced to death for allegedly detonating a bomb amidst a crowd at a demonstration for the eight-hour workday. On November 7, the Bolsheviks took power in Russia and the IWW prisoners celebrated by staging a "battleship," hollering and hooting, cheering and singing, accompanying themselves by banging cups and stools against the iron bars of their cells. When the head jailer threatened to turn the fire hose on them, he was hooted out of the block. On Thanksgiving Day, they protested against the food they were served. Many of the protesters were sent to the uppermost galley in each of the six cell blocks, known as "The Island." It had no lights, only a hint of heat, and was said to be just a step from the nuthouse.

IWW leadership considered various legal strategies. Elizabeth Gurley Flynn suggested that each defendant seek an individual trial, which would put a strain on the system as so many of them would be quite costly as well as cumbersome. The Wobblies had employed the tactic before with some success. Haywood opposed the idea, saying it was contrary to IWW principles. Despite Big Bill's objections, Flynn, Carlo Tresca, and Joe Ettor had their cases tried separately.

The trial of 113 defendants began, with no small degree of irony, on April 1, 1918. On that first day, Arturo Giovannitti protested when his name was not read among the defendants. Upon being told the charges against him had been dropped, he was at first surprised then outraged. Giovannitti scolded the government for not telling him in advance and, thereby, costing him the trip to Chicago from New York. "Another defendant," writes Philip Taft, "A. C. Christ was in army uniform and he was temporarily excused." A dozen defendants were released for one reason or another, leaving 101 to stand trial.

Jury selection took nearly a month. The government claimed the defense used improper methods in determining the views of prospective jurors. Chief prosecutor Frank K. Nebeker set the trial's tone in his opening remarks when he implied the IWW was controlled by an "evil genius." When IWW chief counsel George F. Vanderveer demanded to know the name of this evil genius, Nebeker replied: "[T]his is Mr. Haywood." He went on to say Wobbly direct action and sabotage made the IWW a criminal organization.

Haywood was clearly surprised to see his secretary, Elizabeth Serviss, among the first prosecution witnesses. Nebeker asked her what Haywood, "the king of the movement," was paid each week, and she said: "Ninety dollars."

"What are you paid, Miss Serviss?"

"Eighteen dollars," she replied.

The difference in their salaries was lauded as compelling evidence of the union's inherent hypocrisy. Another witness for the prosecution claimed defendant John Avila had attempted to talk him out of joining the army. A government agent testified that John Baldazzi did not believe in the US government.

"Do you mean Mr. Baldazzi does not believe the government exists?"

"No," the agent replied. "He knows it exists. He just doesn't recognize its authority."

W. W. Wallister, a reporter who had covered the Butte strike, testified that Frank Little had publicly and bitterly referred to US soldiers as "armed thugs" and "Pershing's yellow legs." The epithets provoked disorder in the courtroom. Judge Kenesaw Mountain Landis banged his gavel and threatened to have the room cleared if any more outbreaks should occur.

John Reed and Art Young covered the Chicago trial for the *Liberator* and Reed leaves this description of Judge Landis: "Small on the huge bench sits a wasted man with untidy white hair, an emaciated face in which two burning eyes are set like jewels, parchment skin split by a crack for a mouth; the face of Andrew Jackson three years dead."

Under Ralph Chaplin's editorship, *Solidarity* had printed a number of anticapitalist war editorials that spoke of such wars as not worth fighting because workers foot the bills and fill the graveyards while "parasites get all the gains." Most of these editorials appeared before the United States entered the war in Europe, but the prosecution focused on one that appeared on May 12, 1917. Much was also made of a group of iron ore miners in Crosby, Minnesota, Augusta, Kansas, and Miami, Arizona, submitting antiwar resolutions to IWW headquarters in Chicago. The government used this information to argue that the IWW General Executive Board, under Frank Little's leadership, expelled union members who joined the armed forces. Vanderveer attempted to explain the reasoning behind the policy, but Judge Landis disallowed his argument. Several service men testified in uniform that many IWW members opposed the war. Frank Wernke, who had joined the union as a harvest worker, told the court Wobblies had destroyed farm equipment and employed violence against any worker who refused to join the union.

The prosecution turned its attention to the matter of sabotage. There were literally thousands of saw mills out West, but only two broken saws were submitted as evidence of sabotage. As for the threshing machines so common to the prairie, only six were submitted as the victims of violence. In general terms, the spectrum of what sabotage may mean to a Wobbly runs from "passive resistance" to the violent destruction of property. Testifying for the defense, J. T. (Red) Doran offered some interesting specifics on the IWW's definition of sabotage.[3]

Q. Why isn't cutting logs short sabotage?

A. Because the only thing they succeed in doing by cutting logs short is in disorganizing the orders that the companies have. They do not waste any material which is like the hog. All of the log is used. It is simply if they have orders. For a certain sized material, it may tend to disorganize. Their order system; that is all, but there is no loss, no unusual loss attendant.

Q. Did you ever say anything on the subject of fouling a gear?

A. No.

Q. Or a line?

A. No. You mean—well, I heard this witness here say something about fouling a line.

Q. Well, did you ever—

A. Say anything like that?

Q. Make any comment about a line?

A. Absolutely nothing of that kind.

Q. Is that sabotage?

A. Certainly not.

Q. What is it?

A. That is murder.

Vanderveer at no time accepted any of the government's claims, but argued instead that such meager evidence did not prove the existence of a conspiracy. Defense counsel was not alone in his criticism of the government's weak case; a group of distinguished writers, including Helen Keller, John Dewey, and Thorstein Veblen, voiced similar views. In an effort to ensure a fair trial, the group signed a letter asking for financial aid from the public. The cost to the defense of bringing witnesses to Chicago from all over the country was particularly heavy.

The letters of C. L. Lambert, who was a Wobbly GEB member and secretary of the Defense Committee for Richard (Blackie) Ford and Herman Suhr (both men were convicted of murders occurring during the Wheatland struggle), were entered into evidence.[4] In a letter to Vincent St. John of September 22, 1914, Lambert "boasted that the reduced hop crop in California was the result of IWW sabotage." The defense committee had circulated stickers reading: "AS LONG AS FORD AND SUHR ARE IN PRISON BEWARE OF ALL CALIFORNIA CANNED GOODS" and "DON'T PUT COPPER TACKS IN FRUIT TREES OR ON VINES, IT HURTS THEM."

The prosecution concluded its case and the defense called its first witness: James P. Thompson, one of the founding members of the IWW. Nebeker's interrogation included the usual questions about Wobbly ideology, but the witness was also asked about free love. We can probably credit those questions, apart from their sensationalist value for the prosecution, to rumors about Haywood's carnal exploits in New York. Apparently it was widely believed among the union's inner circle that in those days Big Bill had trouble keeping his fly buttoned. Needless to say, Vanderveer objected to the questions as irrelevant.

Nebeker responded: "Your Honor, the state is simply attempting to establish the defendants' moral character." The judge let the questions stand. There followed a short discussion between prosecutor and witness as to what exactly the term "free love" meant, the content of which brought forth titters and laughter from some spec-

tators. The judge banged his gavel and bellowed: "Ladies and gen-
tleman, this is your last warning." Doesn't the prosecution deeming
it necessary to create such an atmosphere in prosecuting a suppos-
edly airtight case betray the weakness of the case in question?

Wobbly after Wobbly testified to having neither written nor
spoken against the war since the United States became a combatant. Sixty-one defendants took the stand in all. The court was
treated to one lecture on political economy, complete with black-
board and chalk drawings to illustrate key points, and many de-
scriptions by harvest workers, miners, and factory hands of the
conditions under which they toiled. Their testimony managed to
put a great deal into the record of what the judge had previously
ruled irrelevant. Vanderveer also attempted to introduce into evidence the *Report of the Commission on Industrial Relations*, a study appointed by President Woodrow Wilson. The prosecution objected
calling the *Report* "the Bible of the IWW." After a full day of arguments, the judge ruled the evidence was not pertinent to the case.

The defense assembled an impressive list of character witnesses. Forest rangers praised western Wobblies as firefighters.
Farmers said they were hard working and reliable. Mayor Wallace
M. Short of Sioux City, Iowa, and E. F. Blaine, public service com-
missioner for the State of Washington, both testified to Wobblies
being law abiding and peace loving. A number of Philadelphia
longshoreman spoke of IWW workers moving supplies for the
army quartermaster general.

A substantial portion of the courtroom spectators had been
patiently waiting to hear Big Bill Haywood's testimony and watch
the sparks fly when he and the prosecutor locked horns. These

people did not receive the performance they had anticipated. When called to the witness stand, Haywood spoke so softly the judge had to tell him to speak louder. He told the court of his days with the WFM. Nebeker tried to convince the court that Haywood was the "evil genius" behind the violence and destruction of property connected to the Coeur d'Alene strikes of 1892 and 1899. He even insinuated Haywood's guilt in the murder of Frank Steunenberg despite Big Bill having been acquitted of the charge. The prosecutor tried to make something sinister of a marked increase in IWW membership since the war began, but the witness countered by pointing to the American Federation of Labor's even larger wartime membership growth. Haywood likewise denied the IWW was an organization opposed to the war. Nebeker pounced on the denial, asking how Big Bill accounted for the resolutions against the war submitted by IWW locals in Augusta, Kansas, Crosby, Minnesota, and Miami, Arizona, the last of which was sent by Frank Little. Haywood replied, "Little did not represent the organization in his attitude on the war and conscription." One might more accurately say Little did not represent the attitude of Haywood and his predominantly eastern followers; in the letter written to Little, referred to earlier in these pages, Haywood acknowledged that a "good many" of the union's rank and file shared the hobo agitator's position on the war.

The Chicago trial was, at the time, the longest criminal trial in American history, but it took the jury just one hour to find 101 defendants guilty on four counts of conspiracy related to work against the war effort. Vanderveer asked for a new trial on the grounds that the jury had reached 404 decisions far too rapidly, but the judge overruled him. Landis said he believed "the jury could have done nothing else on this evidence but find a verdict of guilty."

Sentencing took place on August 31, 1918, which was also Ralph Chaplin's thirty-first birthday. It took four hours. Five of the defendants received no prison time, two of them got a year and a day in federal prison, thirty-three received five years, another thirty-three got ten years, and fifteen defendants, including Haywood and Chaplin, were given the maximum penalty of twenty years.

Prosecutor Nebeker praised the jury for its intelligence and good judgment. But after perusing the trial's record, forty-four thousand typewritten pages, attorney Alexander Lanier, a captain in the Military Intelligence Division of the Army General Staff, felt the evidence against the defendants was "abysmally inadequate."

In 1918, standard procedure required the segregation of jail prisoners waiting to begin a prison sentence. The Wobblies presented a particular problem as there were ninety-five of them bound for the federal penitentiary at Leavenworth, Kansas. When the day of departure arrived, the route from Cook County Jail to the LaSalle Street Depot, where a special train awaited its cargo, was lined on both sides by policemen. Ralph Chaplin refers to the train as "antiquated day coaches." The prisoners were chained together in groups of three. The trip took twenty-four hours.

# CHAPTER FIVE
# Big Bill Haywood and Frank Little

Born in 1879, Frank Little was ten years younger than Bill Haywood. A full decade his junior, Little could be thought of as Haywood's younger brother, or Big Bill could be described as the hobo agitator's spiritual father. Haywood was a living legend. Unlike the four Haymarket martyrs of 1887, who were hanged in Cook County Jail (one of the original five committed suicide), Haywood was acquitted of murder charges by an Idaho jury. Along with fellow WFM leaders, George Pettibone and Charles H. Moyer, Haywood had been arrested in Colorado for the murder of former Idaho Governor Frank Steunenberg and immediately taken by special train to death row in an Idaho State Prison. The victim had championed labor while running for office, but after the WFM helped get him

143

elected, Steunenberg turned on the union. In response to the killing, Governor Frank Gooding appointed James H. Hawley and William Borah, both of whom had faced the WFM leaders in court in 1899, to investigate the murder. James McParland, head of the Pinkerton Detective Agency in Denver, was hired to lead the investigation. He already had a formidable reputation, having worked as a company spy and infiltrated the "Molly Maguires" before serving as a principal witness in several successful murder trials against them. A team of attorneys, among them Clarence Darrow, defended Haywood, Moyer, and Pettibone.

The three defendants were tried separately. The weekend before Haywood's trial began, rallies and parades took place in several cities. In Boston, union members marching fifty abreast staged a three-hour parade. Nearly one hundred thousand were on hand for a demonstration at Boston Common; the greatest demonstration the Hub has ever witnessed, according to the *Boston Traveler*. President Theodore Roosevelt called Haywood "an undesirable citizen," and in New York large numbers of protesters took to the streets, many of them wearing buttons reading "I am an Undesirable Citizen." According to J. Anthony Lukas, in his fine study, *Big Trouble: Murder in a Small Western Town*, among many "trade unionists there was profound skepticism that Chicagoans would join such a protest, particularly when it was conceived as an open affront to Theodore Roosevelt." A motion was made to purchase fifty thousand "I am an Undesirable Citizen" buttons, but it was not thought so many would be needed and instead only five thousand were ordered. Yet a sizable number of Chicago protesters did carry signs, which read: "I am an undesirable citizen, but Teddy Roosevelt wants my vote." In San Francisco marchers and police clashed, while in New York twenty thousand filled the streets singing their version of "Hold the Fort":

When you look upon your babies 'round your hearthstone
 Bright
Think of Haywood's tear-face daughter, think of her
 Tonight
Make a vow to God in heaven, to that God on high,
That these boys in Idaho by greed shall never die.

As a working miner and fellow WFM organizer, Frank Little was no doubt among those many workers, young and old, who looked up to Big Bill. He was, after all, a workingman who had butted heads with the Big Boys and lived to tell about it.

At age twenty-one, Frank Little was already a member of the Arizona WFM. Three years later, he was agitating—organizing copper miners. Agitating and organizing are, perhaps, not always so closely connected as they were for Little and other western Wobblies. An agitator can most objectively be defined as, according to *Webster's New World Dictionary*, "an apparatus for shaking and stirring, as in a washing machine." I believe this definition carries figurative as well as empirical weight. Little was part of a washing machine charged with the unpopular task of revealing some of capitalist America's dirtiest laundry. When we define organizing objectively, structure and complexity take charge: "to provide with an organic structure, esp. a) to arrange in an orderly way . . . to make into a whole with unified and coherent relationships . . . to

make plans and arrange for . . . to bring into being; establish."
One could easily categorize Frank Little an agitator and Bill Haywood an organizer.

Haywood's prowess as an orator, along with his living legend status, made him effective in both roles. It has been said that Little could not compete with Big Bill as a public speaker, at least not with a crowd expecting the ear-catching phrases for which Haywood was known, some of which include: "The manager's brains are under the workman's cap"; "Twelve hours is a bad habit. Get the Eight-Hour Habit"; "To the Working Class there is no foreigner but the capitalist"; "A shorter day means bigger pay." When asked if he was a Marxist, Haywood would reply: "I've never read Marx's *Capital*, but I have the marks of capital all over me."

Perhaps most importantly, Haywood made his public reputation as an orator speaking to large, sometimes massive, gatherings in the East, while Little's western audience—oftentimes on street corners, in alleys, or outside a tavern—was far smaller. What we have of his speeches up through 1916 is typically western: blunt and to the point. But the difference in their oratorical skills plays only a secondary role in Little being primarily an agitator rather than an organizer. Occasionally he seems less interested in the latter; perhaps because the digging in required of an organizer was at odds with a nomadic life. He travelled light—collected no books, maintained no office, carried a suitcase when feasible and, in his last years, probably a gun. The ore dock strike in 1913 shows him as both agitator and organizer. Otherwise, before 1914, the name "hobo agitator" neatly describes Frank Little's principal function as a Wobbly.

In his autobiography, Big Bill calls himself a violent kid who liked a good fight. While Frank's boyhood is virtually unknown to us, we do know that, as the son of a Quaker, he would have been exposed early on to pacifist beliefs. Our record of his activities contains two noteworthy incidents so far as violence is concerned. First, we have James P. Cannon's report of his walk with Little during the Mesabi ore dock strike on company property patrolled by gun-toting guards. Frank was carrying a pistol. When Cannon asked him why, Frank said he wanted to show the strikers he was not afraid so they wouldn't be afraid. His desire to decrease the strikers' fear of pistol-packing guards could be interpreted as a first step toward preparing them for armed struggle, but his public statements and activities offer no evidence of Little advocating violence. Second, Little was among those charged with murder during the Mesabi conflict in 1916. We could employ a where-there's-smoke-there's-fire attitude toward his arrest, but in my view such a stance too readily overlooks a compelling fact: Little was released after the preliminary hearing for lack of concrete evidence, despite the vicious anti-IWW campaign being carried on by the local press. What has been too often interpreted as a Wobbly propensity for violence could be assessed, says Philip S. Foner, as "a genius for improvising new tactics during the course of a struggle, thus continually setting new fashions in strike tactics." As a strike tactician, Frank Little consistently tested the accepted boundaries, thereby leaving himself open to charges of having gone too far.

Haywood became a miner at age fifteen. On August 10, 1896, after listening to WFM president Ed Boyce speak for three nights in a row, he joined the miners' union. The WFM was only three years old, and Haywood quickly rose through its ranks. Little also advanced rapidly, joining in 1900 and beginning to organize Arizona copper miners three years later. In August 1907, a month after Haywood's acquittal in the Boise trial, Little sided with the IWW against the WFM and was subsequently expelled from the latter. He had taken a stand in opposition to a strictly electoral approach to political action. Given the inherent conflict between capital and labor, how could an electoral system created and controlled by capitalists provide an avenue for labor's best interests?

On June 27, 1905, Haywood presided over the founding convention of the Industrial Workers of the World. Daniel DeLeon, Mother Jones, Eugene V. Debs, and Haymarket martyr Albert Parsons's widow Lucy were also on hand. According to Ed Boyce, the WFM had been "born in jail." The IWW carried on this tradition. While Haywood was incarcerated in Idaho, he claims to have "tackled" the writings of Voltaire, Laurence Sterne, Tolstoy, and Victor Hugo as well as historical classics like Buckle's *History of Civilization* and Draper's *Intellectual History of Europe*. Much of the reading cited above had to have been extremely challenging for a man with a decidedly limited formal education. Following his release after sixteen months in prison, and his subsequent fame, Haywood became a central attraction, the reigning proletariat guru, at Mabel Dodge's salons in New York. Dodge writes of him: "Haywood, so impassioned a speaker out in the rain before a thousand strikers," talked, when asked "easy questions" about the IWW ideology by Walter Lippmann, "as though he was wading blindfolded in sand. . . . Bill's lid drooped over his blind eye and his heavy cheeks sagged lower." Georges Sorel might respond to Dodge's comments by pointing out that men with only elementary educations "imagine that they must have a great deal to learn from authors whose names are so often mentioned with praise in the newspapers" and, we might add, are oftentimes too easily overawed by said authors.

Perhaps Big Bill's insecurities about his own intellectual capabilities contributed to his chastising, albeit justified, remarks concerning Frank Little's misuse, by way of overuse, of the term *son of a bitch*. Ralph Chaplin vividly describes the incident. The IWW had just decided to print some three million stickerettes for May Day 1917. "With his characteristic crooked smile, Little said, 'If we don't hit the bull's eye this time, it won't be our fault. . . . You may be sure there will be one of the silent agitators [stickerettes] on every son of a bitch of a boxcar, water tank, stick handle, and pitchfork in the land on May Day.'" According to Chaplin, a Wobbly poet and intellectual, the GEB generally overused "son of a bitch" despite Haywood's disapproval. Big Bill felt that "constant repetition of the phrase weakened an otherwise useful epithet. "Will you tell me," he demanded, "what words you will use to define a real son of a bitch when you meet one?'"

By that point of course, with the United States already in the war, tensions between Haywood and Little were running dangerously hot. Frank jokingly complained about Haywood's consolidation of power into his own hands, and his seemingly constant directives. To Chaplin, Little said, "When Bill makes up his mind about a thing, we are all supposed to toe the line. And we do—or try to—even to the point of not drinking whiskey. Bill calls that teamwork." Haywood may have been running the IWW in an overbearing manner, but when military conscription was instituted he could not make up his mind how to respond to it, or perhaps felt he could no longer safely speak his mind.

Chaplin describes an earlier incident that displayed Little's near illiteracy. At the union's Chicago headquarters in the autumn of 1915, Haywood asked Little to read Joe Hill's last letter to members of the inner circle. According to Chaplin, when Frank read aloud he habitually stumbled along. One cannot help but wonder if Haywood's request did not have the express purpose of putting a troublesome critic in his place. We must remember that Little's lack of confidence with the printed word would have been shared by most of the migratory laborers he worked with, which is why stickerettes with a picture and caption or catchy little jingle were used to organize throughout the migratory worker's world.

As a veteran member of the GEB and a fierce opponent of Haywood's decision to abandon the free-speech fights, Little was rapidly becoming to the western Wobbly what Haywood was to his counterpart back east. Frank's finger was on the pulse of the United Front at a grassroots level, a level Big Bill Haywood was no longer in touch with. Frank Little's hands-on, direct-action approach to his work was strictly decentralist. He kept no office, viewing offices as part of a centralist landscape. I suspect that after he closed down the free-speech struggle, a significant number of western Wobblies came to see Big Bill Haywood as resting on past laurels. The badly outnumbered westerners fought back as best they could. Thanks in large part to Little's work with the AWO and the United Front, the numbers and revenue gap separating the union's eastern and western branches started to shrink. When the war in Europe began, Frank Little and the western Wobblies were rising stars. They possessed a sense of independence not enjoyed by the eastern factory worker.

For us, today, a rivalry between Haywood and Little may too easily appear to be a one-sided affair, motivated by envy on the latter's part. After all, John Reed had not passionately described Frank addressing strikers; nor is Frank featured in Warren Beatty's epic film, *Reds*; nor is Frank said to be the model for the protagonist in Jack London's classic novel, *The Iron Heel.* But if we stand back for a minute, and consider Frank Little's impact on the lives of nameless workers by the thousands unacquainted with Reed's article in *The Masses*, at a time before Beatty and his film, I think we can see Little's considerable and hard-earned status in radical labor's pantheon.

In any case, the success of the AWO 400, in which Frank played a leading role, must at first have been greeted by Haywood with open arms because the IWW needed more members and more money. But that success quickly proved threatening to Big Bill. Little was the leading exponent of an antiwar general strike and, worse yet for Haywood, the AWO 400 supported the hobo agitator's position. Haywood was under a lot of pressure. Was he jealous of Little's popularity and influence in the AWO, figuring those men and other western and southern Wobblies, a rapidly growing number, believed Frank Little to be a Wobbly in full, of word and deed alike, while Big Bill was, by that point in his life, "more show than go"?

Haywood publicly declared war on the Steel Trust in 1916, but did not go to the Mesabi Range battlefield, not even to inspect the troops—a fact duly noted by the Duluth *News Tribune*. His courage was also brought into question by Alexander Berkman, Emma Goldman's lover, who had spent many years in prison as a failed as-

sassin. Haywood also refused to participate in a funeral, organized
by Berkman and Goldman, for three anarchists who had conspired
to kill John D. Rockefeller. He feared the event might lead to more
repression. Berkman said of Big Bill: "In later years he had repeatedly shown the white feather." A Wobbly defense attorney called
Haywood jumping bail and fleeing to Russia "the act of a coward."
Of course, unlike the attorney, Haywood had already twice served
eighteen-month stretches, first on death row in Idaho, then in
Leavenworth, Kansas. He knew prison life first-hand and, consequently, feared dying in one to a degree the attorney quite probably
could not comprehend. At age fifty with a twenty-year sentence,
Big Bill was a good prospect to end his days in prison.

The pressure exerted by the US entry into the war must have
been quite a load for Big Bill Haywood. I cannot help wondering if
he occasionally loathed the burden of being 'Big Bill.' A politician
as Frank Little never was, Haywood tended to tighten his grip
under pressure. He disciplined Elizabeth Gurley Flynn and Carlo
Tresca for their mishandling of the 1916 Mesabi strike. The two
had advised the defendants to plea bargain. Flynn and Tresca subsequently left the IWW. The break had been coming since 1914,
when Flynn and Tresca sided with Frank Little against Haywood
during the debates on the free-speech actions. Little was loyal to his
friends, so when Flynn needed a board member on her side, he
spoke up. Chaplin writes: "Even after war had been declared, he
[Little] fought to the last ditch for reprinting Elizabeth Gurley
Flynn's *Sabotage*, a pamphlet describing a type of sabotage advocated by European anarchists and syndicalists from which the
IWW had adopted only a few features applicable to conditions in

the USA." The form of Wobbly sabotage most commonly advocated was striking on the job with stickerettes and a widely circulated jingle: "The hours are long/ the pay is small/ so take your time/ and buck 'em all." Slow downs and sit-downs were the order of the day.

Flynn, Tresca, and Little remained friends for the rest of Little's life. Flynn writes touchingly about Tresca bringing her the news of Little's death: "I felt truly bad about Frank Little, the first friend of mine to meet such a dreadful, violent death. Whenever I visited Butte in after years, I went to his grave out in the flats. It is adorned by a stone erected by the workers of Butte, surrounded by the graves of copper miners."

The hobo agitator's courage would seem to be well established, though the federal government accused him posthumously of threatening and extorting farm laborers. If true, Little might be prematurely described as a bully of spurious courage. Even so, a central question remains: If one cannot hire or force by law soldiers for one's cause, and only so many can be converted through compelling rational arguments, isn't one likely to become a bully? In his statements about "taking a firing squad" and "going out in a blaze of glory" an apocalyptic consciousness can be detected for which a term like "bully" has little meaning, as a "death before dishonor" frame of mind appears to be firmly in place. In any event, the actions for which Little might be labeled a bully stem from two objectives: one, building as rapidly as possible a massive base for a general strike against the war; two, following basic AWO 400 policy.

# CHAPTER SIX
# Three Western Wobbly Martyrs

Patrick Renshaw's *The Wobblies: The Story of Syndicalism in the United States* devotes a twenty-five-page chapter to three Wobbly martyrs. Significantly, all three were western Wobblies. Eighteen of those twenty-five pages concern Joe Hill, while Wesley Everest and Frank Little receive four and three pages, respectively. Yet, Renshaw claims Little is a more authentic martyr than Hill. Likewise historian Irving Werstein writes: "Joe Hill had died a 'true-blue rebel' [but] he was far less a real hero than Frank Little. Next to Big Bill Haywood, Frank Little was the most vital leader in the IWW." How did Joe Hill become internationally known, while Frank Little and Wesley Everest slipped into history's footnotes? I think we can attribute much of Hill's status as a martyr to his stature as a working-

class artist. A further-to-the-left Woody Guthrie, Hill was thought
of by politically progressive artists of the time as one of their own—
at least that feeling took effect once he was facing execution and
suddenly big news. Like Sacco and Vanzetti and Julius and Ethel
Rosenberg, for a time the cause of Joe Hill, who was believed to be
unjustly convicted of murder, sent massive crowds into the streets.
Hill's story is well known. He died by firing squad. Utah law gave
the condemned a choice of hanging or firing squad, and Hill chose
the latter. "According to legend," writes Werstein, "[Hill] gave the
command to fire." On the day he died Hill sent a telegram to Haywood, which Frank Little read aloud. The message ended with the
instructive: "Don't waste time mourning. Organize." Joe Hill was
dead, but his songs—"Casey Jones," "The Union Scab," "The Rebel
Girl" (about Elizabeth Gurley Flynn), and "The Preacher and the
Slave"—and many others lived on, according to Werstein, "in picket
lines, in demonstrations, in wheat fields and boxcars, in lumber
camps, mines, and mills."

The United States entered the war in Europe in April 1917, and
Frank Little was lynched on August 1 of that same year. Several
sources mention him saying, during the last months of his life, that
he would prefer a firing squad to knuckling under on the war. One
is tempted to think Little envied Joe Hill going out in "a blaze of
glory," which was a phrase Frank applied to himself during his last
year of life. Hill's execution was carried out by the state with all the
formal decorum required by law while Little's execution had no such
dignity. He was given no choices. He was instead dragged behind a
vehicle, then hanged and, by some accounts, castrated. The manner
of Joe Hill's death was far cleaner than that of Frank Little's. After

all, only the state is allowed to take human life with clean hands. The hands of masked vigilantes are very dirty indeed.

The Joe Hill legend has two components: the clean Joe Hill, executed by the state, who has, by that execution, paid in full for his crimes and Joe Hill, the IWW balladeer. The former might be called the stage upon which the latter performs. Like Sacco and Vanzetti and the Rosenbergs, he is a victim of the justice system, and his stature as an artist-entertainer enriches his martyrdom. Frank Little, on the other hand, had no ready passage into the more glamorous celebrity aspects of American culture. The importance of song to the IWW should not be underestimated. Robert L. Tyler writes, "The I.W.W. probably revealed its character most fully in its songs, for it was famed as a singing organization." The Wobbly songbook has gone through a number of editions. The union set a substantial number of its tunes to church hymns while many of those same songs readily lend themselves to a country-western format as well. Wobbly songs contained a good bit of black humor—the fruit of numerous confrontations with the police, vigilantes, and angry businessmen who enforced the ideals of an allegedly liberal United States.

Like Frank Little, Wesley Everest's life came to an end at the hands of faceless killers. He was hung from the Chehalis River bridge, shot several times and, according to Peter Carlson's account in *Roughneck*, castrated. Everest's body was thrown into a nameless grave. He had not been a Wobbly leader, as Little had, nor a well-known figure like Hill. He was instead a red-card carrying lumberjack who, despite his opposition to the war, joined the army and fought in the trenches of France with the American Expeditionary

Force before returning to America in 1919. By November of that year he was part of a long and bitter lumber strike in Centralia, Washington. By this time President Woodrow Wilson had admitted that "the war to end all wars," "the war to make the world safe for democracy" had in fact been "an industrial and commercial war," which, according to Bill Haywood, earned the United States $30 billion.

In his autobiography Haywood says US secretary of labor William B. Wilson, formerly secretary of the United Mine Workers of America, had "so far as was in his power, outlawed the IWW." Encouraged by the Secretary's stance, the Lumberman's Association, according to Haywood, "proceeded with a campaign of suppression and violence under the guise of law." Big Bill believed Secretary William B. Wilson "made the Centralia tragedy possible." A Red Cross Parade sparked the first Centralia raid in April 1918. Haywood observes that newspapers owned by "'the lumber trusts' fiercely denounced the western Wobblies, speaking of them in terms identical to those used against abolitionists before the Civil War" and igniting a raid on the union hall. Some IWW members were jailed while others were "dumped across the county line." The union made no attempt, according to Haywood, "to defend their hall in this raid, but it was different on Armistice Day."

November 11, 1919, marked the Armistice's first anniversary and the Centralia American Legion post marched on the IWW union hall. Werstein describes the scene: They came with firearms of all sorts, clubs, and "lengths of pipe." The lumber bosses issued a statement from their headquarters in Centralia saying the Wobblies must either "clear out of town or be carried out in a hearse." The outnumbered union men defended their hall; Wesley Everest among them, wearing the uniform he had worn in France. Legend has it he had armed himself with a rifle and a .45, and was heard to say: "I fought for democracy in France, and I'm going to fight for it here." When the Legionnaires entered the hall, he yelled, "Stand where you are. I'll kill the first one who moves." They kept coming, so he emptied the rifle into them and ran out the back door, pistol in hand. He ran into the woods, with Legionnaires in hot pursuit. Everest made his last stand waist deep in the Shookumchuck River; its strong current kept him from crossing. He said he would surrender to the police but not a mob. Dale Hubbard, nephew of the Lumberman's Association's top man, attempted to take him in custody and was shot dead. When a Legionnaire threatened to lynch Everest on the spot, he replied: "You haven't got the guts to hang a man in daylight." That night masked men smashed in the jailhouse door, overpowered the deputy, and dragged Everest from his cell. He is said to have cried out: "Tell the boys I died for my class."

No charges were ever brought against his killers, but hundreds of Wobblies were arrested and eleven held for killing three Legionnaires at the Centralia union hall. By Werstein's account, six of those eleven were sentenced to "twenty-five to forty years in the state penitentiary." Bill Haywood claims five of the jurymen later swore "to affidavits saying that the verdict was unjust" while Werstein writes, "In 1923, nine of the jurors swore under oath that they had reached their verdict under pressure from the lumber bosses and that no one on the jury actually believed the convicted Wobblies had been guilty."

While Wesley Everest is undoubtedly a full-fledged IWW martyr, his lack of prominence in the union may explain his historical
obscurity. The fact that he was wearing his US Army uniform when
he committed the acts that subsequently martyred him puts Everest
in a unique position. Unlike Frank Little, Everest fought in the
"capitalistic slaughter fest" then came home and took up arms in
defense of the IWW's right to exist in a free society. He might easily be considered a more sympathetic figure than Frank Little. But,
from another perspective, Everest's allegiance to the IWW while in
the uniform of his country makes him a turncoat who wishes to
rub his enemies' noses in his disdain for their United States. Everest's actions qualify him as a decided threat to the government. If
other former soldiers turned working men had emulated Everest in
any type of organized fashion, given their war experience and the
sympathy they might well have aroused, their potential for unauthorized violence and possibly a worker-soldier victory are not to be
ignored. Of course, given the wartime hysteria, the possibilities for
such an emulation were very small indeed.

Wesley Everest being in uniform when he was lynched has
other noteworthy aspects. The 1918 Sedition Act made it a crime
to utter, print, write, or publish "any disloyal, profane, scurrilous,
or abusive language about . . . the uniform of the Army or Navy of
the United States, or promote the cause of its enemies." But when
Everest was lynched in uniform, as were a number of black soldiers
just back from the war, the federal government did not intervene.

Everest must certainly have been called a traitor to his class by
some of his fellow Wobblies. So, to redeem himself, he stood that
autumn day prepared for combat: a soldier in defense of his class. By

dying as he did, Everest could be said to have symbolically united the United States and the IWW by making the latter's concept of industrial democracy ("products for all and profits for none") the driving force behind a new nation's military objectives. From the capitalist's viewpoint, such a vision was not to be tolerated. Likewise, Frank Little's influence on a grassroots, Populist, collectivist united front—militant and rapidly growing—had to be terminated.

Finally, Hill and Everest were held to be killers while Frank Little had virtually no record of physical violence, though his words were sometimes accused of provoking it. While an irrational passion engendered by anti-IWW and pro-war hysteria provides a ready explanation for Little being lynched despite his nonviolent ways, it likewise offers a convenient moment for old adversaries seeking to permanently silence an opponent who had been vigorously plaguing them for far too long.

# CONCLUSION
# Frank Little, Where Are You Now that We Need You?

As a staff writer for a Minneapolis-based jazz magazine in the early 1980s, I had the opportunity of interviewing actors Ossie Davis and Ruby Dee. Davis talked about *Buck and the Preacher*, a film Dee had made with Sidney Poitier and Harry Belafonte, in which recently freed black slaves traveling west to claim their forty acres enlist the aid of Native Americans in a fight against land-grabbing racists. Dee reminisced about the couple's annual trips to Saint Paul, Minnesota, to perform at Hamline University. Speaking of the Minneapolis/St. Paul skyline, she said every year it contains "more temples to the Gods in whom we truly believe." Nearly thirty years later, in the shadow of those "temples" and many more like them, I wish to say a few words about Frank Little's relevance for the present moment.

If global capitalism does, as some commentators insist, mark "the end of history," thereby setting the boundaries within which any real change can still be effected (assuming of course *real* change is possible within an environment created by global capitalism), then nurturing resistance, disgruntlement, and discontent rather than allowing these forces to dissipate in a seemingly endless proliferation of diversions (especially those of the pharmaceutical and technological variety) would seem to be of paramount importance. Otherwise, we would risk becoming a nation of "happy slaves" dedicated to the ideals and objectives necessary for the continued "happiness of all those who possess the means of living well."

The term "wage slaves" accurately describes a vast number of working people today. While this term's adjective may, at least in some cases, alleviate a good deal of the sting inflicted by its noun, a particularly insidious form of slavery is nevertheless alive and prospering. As noted leftist historian M. I. Finley writes, "Compulsory labor takes many forms; one of those forms is debt bondage." The rapid growth of said bondage over the last thirty years is common knowledge. The vast majority of Americans' economic situation is aptly stated by a bumper sticker (a modern-day stickerette) that reads: "I owe, I owe, so off to work I go"—if, of course, they are fortunate enough to have a job. The slave who believes he can do nothing but laugh at his own bondage and pull the chains ever tighter in an effort to keep his head above water, is not laughing for joy but as the helpless laugh: at that which is not funny. And this laughter would appear to be essential if the social wheels are to remain well greased.

Little's commitment to testing the boundaries of free speech is still very much needed today. By free speech I mean the articulation and serious discussion of ideas that, if not extinct, are definitely endangered so far as public discourse is concerned. Cultural critic and philosopher Theodor W. Adorno describes the problem thusly: "Almost everything to be read has already been said, commonplace and, by virtue of that fact, untrue. The only things left to say are those that elude saying. Only the most extreme statements have any chance of escaping from the mush of established opinion." While this statement might be interpreted as advocating extremism for its own sake, the commitment I have in mind, and believe Frank Little shared, is to those ideas which are being demonized or ignored entirely; thus, the unspeakable must be spoken and *seriously* discussed. Little spoke the unspeakable: Don't fight in that war in Europe, stay home and fight your real enemies—the bosses. By speaking the unspeakable, saying the unsayable, Frank Little embodied Hannah Arendt's definition of a poet. In an essay on poet and playwright Bertolt Brecht she writes: "a poet [is] . . . someone who must say the unsayable, who must not remain silent on occasions when all are silent, and who must therefore be careful not to talk about things that all talk about."

If we are to blossom in an age of fear, we may very well need to defy the tenets of human nature as they are currently being peddled, tenets that tell us a concept like "products for all profits for none" flies in the face of our nature as human beings. These are the same tenets that tell us greed is a basic human emotion, perfectly natural and therefore perfectly acceptable. But anger, another perfectly natural human emotion, is unacceptable when not in the service of legitimate authority. Why is greed acceptable while anger is closely circumscribed? Who and what most benefits from greed being accepted, and thereby to some extent encouraged, while unauthorized anger is quite often considered a symptom of a pathological condition? Anger management counseling is routinely required by courts of law.

Today we need Frank Little most of all at an elemental, visceral level. We need his yearning and his anger. We need the tenacity of his commitment. Perhaps then a way of living together that raised its head for a few days in the Seattle General Strike of 1919 can once again come into being. American society has certainly reached a point where the Left has nothing to lose by asserting itself rather than simply accommodating what we're so frequently told is inevitable. The questions Wobbly poet Arturo Giovannitti asked the ruling class in 1917 are in some ways even more germane today:

Shall now the pent-up spirit no longer connive
  with the sun against your midnight?
And are we now all reconciled to your rule
  are you safer and we humbler, and is the night
  eternal and the day forever blotted out of the
  skies,
And all blind yesterdays risen, and all tomorrows entombed

# ACKNOWLEDGMENTS

I wish to thank Charles A. Rankin for offering me encouragement when I needed it most; Michael C. Jordan for his invaluable help with practical matters; Thomas F. Dillingham and Robert Hollinger for their encouragement and advice; Julie Herrara for reading an early draft of the manuscript; Alan Maass and Dao X. Tran for their invaluable suggestions; and my partner in life, Delores Kay Stead, for things too numerous to mention. I also wish to thank the Joseph A. Labadie Collection for allowing me to draw on their vast holdings.

# Sources

## BOOKS AND ESSAYS

Aaron, Daniel. *Writers on the Left: Episodes in American Literary Communism.* Columbia University Press, New York: 1992.

Arblaster, Anthony. *Democracy.* Open University Press, Buckingham and Philadelphia: 2002.

Arendt, Hannah. "Bertolt Brecht: 1898–1956" in *Men in Dark Times.* Harcourt, Brace, & World, Inc., New York: 1955, 207–249.

———. "Reflections on Violence," in *Anthology: Selected Essays from Thirty Years of The New York Review of Books.* Edited by Robert B. Silvers and Barbara Epstein. New York Review of Books Press, New York: 2001.

Bakunin, Michael. *God and the State.* Dover Publications, Inc., New York: 1970.

Benjamin, Walter. "Critique of Violence" in *Walter Benjamin: Selected Writings: Volume 1 1913–1926.* Translated by Edmund Jephcott.

236-252. Harvard University Press, Cambridge, MA: 1996.

Bird, Stewart, Georgakas, Dan, and Shaffer, Deborah. *Solidarity Forever: An Oral History of the IWW*. Lake View Press, Chicago: 1985.

Bourne, Randolph S. *War and the Intellectuals: Collected Essays 1915–1919*. Edited by Carl Resek. Hackett Publishing Company, Inc., Indianapolis Cambridge: 1964.

Boyer, Richard O. and Morias, Herbert M. *Labor's Untold Story*. United Electrical, Radio and Machine Workers of America, Pittsburgh: 1955.

Brissenden, Paul Frederick. *The I.W.W.: A Study of American Syndicalism*. P. S. King & Son, Ltd, New York: 1919.

Bush, Charles C. *The Green Corn Rebellion*. Master's thesis, University of Oklahoma, 1932.

Cannon, James P. *Notebook of an Agitator*. Pathfinder Press, New York: 1973.

Carlson, Peter. *Roughneck: The Life and Times of Big Bill Haywood*. W. W. Norton and Company, New York and London: 1983.

Chaplin, Ralph. *Wobbly: The Rough & Tumble Story of an American Radical*. De Capo Press, New York: 1972.

Chrislock, Carl H. *Watchdog of Loyalty: The Minnesota Commission of Public Safety During World War I*. Minnesota Historical Society Press, St. Paul: 1991.

Claussen, Detlev. *Theodor W. Adorno: One Last Genius*. Translated by Rodney Livingstone. Harvard University Press, Cambridge, MA and London: 2008.

Conlin, Joseph Robert. *Bread & Roses Too: Studies of the Wobblies*. Greenwood Publishing Corporation, Westport, CT: 1969.

——. *Bill Haywood and the Radical Labor Movement*. Syracuse University Press, Syracuse, NY: 1969.

Dos Passos, John. *The 42nd Parallel*. Washington Square Press Incorporated, New York: 1961.

Dubofsky, Melvyn. *We Shall Be All: A History of the Industrial Workers of the World*. New York University Press, Binghamton, NY: 1968.

——. *Big Bill Haywood*. University of Manchester Press, Manchester: 1987.

Filler, Louis. *Randolph Bourne*. Citadel Press, New York: 1966.

Finley, M. I. *Ancient Slavery and Modern Ideology*. Viking Press, New York: 1980.

Flynn, Elizabeth Gurley. *I Speak My Own Piece*. Masses & Mainstream: New York: 1955.

Foner, Philip S. *History of the Labor Movement in the United States Vol. IV: The Industrial Workers of the World, 1905–1917*. International Publishers, New York: 1965.

——. *Fellow Workers and Friends: IWW Free-Speech Fights as told by the Participants*. Edited by Philip S. Foner. Greenwood Press, Westpoint, CT: 1981.

Gutfeld, Arnon. "The Murder of Frank Little: Radical Labor Agitation in Butte, Montana, 1917, in *Labor History* 10, no. 2 (1969): 177–92.

Hall, Greg. *The Harvest Wobblies: The Industrial Workers of the World and Agricultural Laborers of the American West, 1905–1930*. Oregon State University Press, Corvallis: 2001.

Hammett, Dashiell. *Red Harvest*. Vintage, New York: 1989.

Haywood, Bill. *Bill Haywood's Book: The Autobiography of William D. Haywood*. International Publishers, New York: 1929.

Hofstadter, Richard. *Anti-Intellectualism in American Life*. Vintage Books, New York: 1964.

Johnson, Diane. *Dashiell Hammett: A Life*. Random House, New York: 1983.

Kornbluh, Joyce L. *Rebel Voices: An I.W.W. Anthology*. University of Michigan Press, Ann Arbor: 1964.

Layman, Richard. *Shadow Man: The Life of Dashiell Hammett*. Harcourt Brace Jovanovich, New York and London: 1981.

Lasch, Christopher. *The True and Only Heaven: Progress and Its Critics*. W. W. Norton and Company, New York and London: 1991.

Leier, Mark. *Bakunin: The Creative Passion*. St. Martin's Press, New York: 2006.

Lukas, J. Anthony. *Big Trouble: A Murder in a Small Western Town Sets Off a Struggle for the Soul of America*. Simon and Schuster, New York: 1997.

Marcuse, Herbert. *Reason and Revolution: Hegel and the Rise of Social Theory*. Beacon Press, Boston: 1960.

Nies, Judith. *Native American History: A Chronology of a Culture's Vast Achievements and Their Links to World Events*. Ballantine Books, New York: 1996.

Nolan, William F. *Hammett: A Life on the Edge*. Congdon and Weed, Inc., New York: 1983.

Paine, Thomas. *Rights of Man*. Penguin Books, New York: 1984.

Parker, Carleton H. *The Casual Laborer and Other Essays*. Harcourt Brace and Howe, New York: 1920.

Phillips, Kevin. *Wealth and Democracy: A Political History of the American Rich*. Broadway Books, New York: 2002.

Preston, William. *Aliens and Dissenters: Federal Suppression of Radicals*. Harvard University Press, Cambridge: 1963.

Renshaw, Patrick. *The Wobblies: The Story of Syndicalism in the United States*. Doubleday & Company, Garden City, NY: 1967.

Schwoegler, Steve. "Frank Little, Where Are You Now That We Need You?" *Industrial Worker*. July 1982, 5.

Sellars, Nigel Anthony. *Oil, Wheat, and Wobblies: The Industrial Workers of the World in Oklahoma, 1905–1930*. University of Oklahoma Press, Norman: 1998.

Sorel, Georges. *The Illusions of Progress*. Translated by John and Charlotte Stanley. University of California Press, Berkeley: 1972.

——. *Reflections on Violence*. Translated by T. E. Hulme and J. Roth. Free Press, Glencoe, IL: 1950.

Taft, Philip. "The Federal Trials of the IWW," *Labor History* 3, Winter, 1962, 57–91.

Thompson, E. P. *The Making of the English Working Class*. Pantheon, New York: 1964.

Tyler, Robert L. "I.W.W. in the Pacific N.W.: Rebels of the Woods," *Ore-*

*gon Historical Quarterly* 55, no. 1 (March 1954): 3–44.

——. "The I.W.W. and the West," *American Quarterly* 12, no. 2, part 1 (Summer 1960): 175–87.

Wald, Alan M. *The New York Intellectuals: The Rise and Decline of the Anti-Stalinist Left from the 1930s to the 1980s.* University of North Carolina Press, Chapel Hill and London: 1987.

Weber, Max. *The Protestant Ethic and the Spirit of Capitalism.* Translated by Talcott Parsons. Routledge, New York and London: 1992.

Werstein, Irving. *Pie in the Sky, an American Struggle: The Wobblies and Their Times.* Delacorte Press, New York: 1969.

Williams, William Appleton. *The Contours of American History.* W. W. Norton and Company, New York and London: 1988.

Zinn, Howard. *A People's History of the United States: 1492–Present.* HarperCollins, New York: 2001.

# Notes

## INTRODUCTION

1.  Hammett's first novel, *Red Harvest,* is narrated by a Pinkerton-like operative involved in a labor dispute and plenty of violence in a place called Poisonville (read: Butte).
2.  University of Oklahoma Press editor Charles Rankin in private correspondence.

## CHAPTER ONE: THE WESTERN WOBBLIES

1.  "Scissor Bill" was one of Joe Hill's most popular songs and appeared in the *Industrial Worker* on February 16, 1913. It is sung to the tune of "Steamboat Bill." The lyrics are as follows:

You may ramble round the country anywhere you will,
You'll always run across the same old Scissor Bill.
He's found upon the desert, he is upon the hill,
He's found in every mining camp and lumber mill,
He looks just like a human, he can eat and walk,
But you will find he isn't, when he starts to talk.
He'll say, "This is my country," with an honest face,
While all the cops they chase him out of every place.
Chorus:
*Scissor Bill, he is a little dippy,*
*Scissor Bill, he has a funny face.*
*Scissor Bill should drown in Mississippi,*
*He is the missing link that Darwin tried to trace.*


And Scissor Bill he couldn't live without the booze,
He sits around all day and spits tobacco juice.
He takes a deck of cards and tries to beat the Chink!
Yes, Bill would be a smart guy if he could only think,
And Scissor Bill he says: "This country must be freed
From Niggers, Jews, and Dutchmen and the gol durn Swede."

Chorus:
*Scissor Bill, the "foreigners" is cussin;*
*Scissor Bill, he says "I hate a Coon";*
*Scissor Bill is down on everybody*
*The Hottentots, the bushmen and the man in the moon.*


Don't try to talk your union dope to Scissor Bill,
He says he never organized and never will,
He'll always be satisfied until he's dead,
With coffee and a doughnut and a lousy old bed.
And Bill, he says he gets rewarded thousand fold,

When he gets up to heaven on the streets of gold.
But I don't care who knows it, and right here I'll tell.If Scissor
    Bill is going to heaven, I'll go to Hell.
Chorus:
*Scissor Bill, wouldn't join the union,*
*Scissor Bill, he says, "Not me, by Heck!"*
*Scissor Bill gets his reward in Heaven,*
*Oh! sure. He'll get it, but he'll get it in the neck*

2. An "anything's better than wages" ethos reverberates throughout the westerner's search for freedom and is a prominent motif in films about modern-day cowboys like Sam Peckinpah's *Junior Bonner* and John Huston's *The Misfits.*

3. The friction between reform and revolution is too often portrayed as both inevitable and debilitating for both causes. But it need not be either, as a desire for reform can become a desire for revolution if properly nurtured.

4. In his preface to *Humanism and Terror*, Maurice Merleau-Ponty observes: "The purity of principles not only tolerates but even requires violence. Thus there is a mystification in liberalism." Drawing on Marx's *Critique of Hegel's Philosophy of the Right*, Merleau-Ponty argues that "liberal ideas belong to a system of violence," and within that system function as the "general basis of consolation and justification."

5. Arendt's distinction between action and behavior gains additional significance when we consider it in relation to Hegel's well-known remark about thinking: "Thinking is, indeed, essentially the negation of that which is immediately before us." In *Reason and Revolution: Hegel and the Rise of Social Theory*, Herbert Marcuse expresses a concern that "the power of negative thinking [is] in danger of being obliterated."

6. "Half-Indian, Half-White Man, and All-Wobbly" is the phrase one most frequently encounters as a way of nut-shelling Frank Little, a fact that should come as no surprise during an era when identity politics has largely replaced class consciousness.

7.   Carlton H. Parker managed to be distrusted by unions, migratory
     workers, and management. Neither a typical academic nor a bureau-
     crat, Parker was a journalist and a bond trader. He served for a time
     as the executive secretary of the State Immigration and Housing
     Commission, taught economics at the University of California-San
     Francisco and later at the University of Washington. See *An Ameri-
     can Idyll: The Life of Carlton H. Parker* by Cornelia Stratton Parker
     (Atlantic Monthly Press, New York: 1920).

8.   In middle-class politics with its emphasis on certainty and stability
     one's platform is to be presented in "subtle detail." Those Wobblies
     under the influence of Georges Sorel, or kindred spirits of those
     who were, formed a sizable portion of the union. They wished to
     break free from middle-class politics and cared little or nothing
     about "subtle details."

9.   Paternalism seeks not only to control, but likewise presumes igno-
     rance on the part of those being parented. The IWW educa-
     tional/communal function, discussed by Joseph Conlin and Nigel
     Sellars, must have been especially disturbing to the capitalist class;
     for the Wobblies were encouraging those too busy surviving to have
     time for book learning to put their minds to work. For a fascinating
     study of similar efforts in Great Britain see Jonathan Rose, *The In-
     tellectual Life of the British Working Classes* (Yale University Press, New
     Haven and London: 2001).

10.  If many of those who lit out for the Territory were, like Huck Finn,
     running away from being "sivilized," shouldn't we at least briefly pon-
     der Freud's famous statement that civilization is both the cure *and* the
     cause of humankind's problems? What might that contemplation ren-
     der visible about civilization and Sorel's version of progress?

## CHAPTER TWO: FREE-SPEECH FIGHT

1. According to Carlton H. Parker's report on the Wheatland Riot, says Kornbluh's *Rebel Voices*, "the sheriff and his deputies fired into a group of 2000 strikers who were singing 'Mr. Block'. . . . The song inspired Ernest Riebe's popular series of 'Mr. Block' cartoons which appeared in *Solidarity*, *The Industrial Worker*, and other I.W.W. publications."

### MR. BLOCK
By Joe Hill
(Tune: "It Looks to Me Like a Big Time Tonight")

Please give me your attention, I'll introduce to you
A man that is a credit to "Our Red, White and Blue;"
His head is made of lumber, and solid as a rock;
He is a common worker and his name is Mr. Block.
And Block thinks he may be President some day.

Chorus:
*Oh, Mr. Block you were born a mistake,*
*You take the cake,*
*You make me ache.*
*Tie a rock on your block and then jump in the lake,*
*Kindly do that for liberty's sake.*

Yes, Mr. Block is lucky; he found a job, by gee!
The shark got seven dollars, for job and fare and fee.
They shipped him to the desert and dumped him with his truck,
But when he tried to find his job he sure was out of luck.
He shouted, "That's too raw, I'll fix them with the law."
Block hiked back to the city, but wasn't doing well.

He said, "I'll join the union—the great A.F. of L."
He got a job next morning, got fired in the night,
He said, "I'll see Sam Gompers and he'll fix that foreman right."
Sam Gompers said, "You see, You've got my sympathy."
Election Day he shouted, "A Socialist for Mayor!"
The "comrade" got elected, he happy was for fair,
And after the election he got an awful shock,
A great big Socialist Bull did rap him on his block.
And Comrade Block did sob, "I helped him to his job."
Poor Block he died one evening, I'm very glad to state;
He climbed the golden ladder up to the pearly gate.
He said, "Oh, Mr. Peter, one word I'd like to tell,
I'd like to meet the Asterbilts and John D. Rocke-fell."
Old Pete said, "Is that so? You'll meet them down below."

Note the song's distrust, a là Georges Sorel, for the opportunistic Socialist politician.

2.  During the period of Little's stay in Fresno his brother W. F. was arrested on October 22 for being drunk in public and pled not guilty. On October 24 he begged the judge for mercy, saying he had a wife and family to support and could not afford any more jail time. He also promised to quit the IWW. The judge thereupon suspended his ninety-day sentence. W. F. was four years older than Frank and had been working in a carpet cleaning plant at the time of his arrest.

3.  Roger Bruns, *The Damndest Radical: The Life and World of Ben Reitman, Chicago's Celebrated Social Reformer, Hobo King, and Whorehouse Physician* (Chicago: University of Illinois Press, 2001).

4.  Ernst Toller describes the situation from his viewpoint as a German leftist: "In face of the feverish spread of wartime nationalism nobody remembered to think internationally; chauvinism triumphed; the proletariat of every land forgot their oaths of brotherhood and shot each other down. They rushed to the defense not of humanity

but of the capitalistic states; their enemies were no longer the bourgeois but their friends on the other side of the border; the ideals of the past were stronger than those of the future; the instincts so long instilled by the ruling class proved stronger than their transient reasoned ideas" See *I Was a German: The Autobiography of Ernst Toller* (William Morrow and Company, New York: 1934).

## CHAPTER THREE: IRON ORE MINERS, HARVEST HANDS, AND OIL WORKERS

1.  The Duluth *News Tribune* kept a close watch on "labor unrest," reporting in some detail on events throughout an area that included parts of Minnesota, North Dakota, Wisconsin, and Michigan. Apart from the obvious ideological considerations, such reportage must certainly have helped sell newspapers.

2.  See Dorothy Gallagher, *All the Right Enemies: The Life and Murder of Carlo Tresca* (New Brunswick, NJ: Rutgers University Press, 2001); and Nunzio Perricone, *Carlo Tresca: Portrait of a Rebel* (New York: Palgrave Macmillan, 2005).

3.  Ibid.

4.  E. F. Doree was among the defendants in the Chicago conspiracy trial and drew a ten-year prison sentence. See Ellen Doree Rosen, *A Wobbly Life: IWW Organizer E. F. Doree* (Detroit: Wayne State University Press, 2004).

## CHAPTER FOUR: URGENCY AND CONSPIRACY

1.  See Arnon Gutfield, "The Murder of Frank Little."

2.  In a union not short on poets, Arturo Giovannitti was probably the

most accomplished. See his English-language collection, *Arrows in the Gale* (Riverside, CT: Hillacre Bookhouse, 1914), with an introduction by Helen Keller.

3.   In a letter of Peter Stone's to Joyce Kornbluh, dated February 3, 1964: "Red Doran was a West Coast soapboxer who had quite a following in Seattle in 1916–18. By trade he was an electrician, but he would rather soapbox or give 'chart talks' than work at the trade."

4.   Richard (Blackie) Ford and Herman Suhr, the former described as "quite eloquent" while the latter is by some dubbed "slightly retarded," were convicted of second-degree murder. The prosecution admitted neither man was at the scene of the killing, but claimed they had provoked others to murder. The two men were sentenced to life terms. They were pardoned in 1924.

# Index

© Amanda Wright

## ABOUT THE AUTHOR

Arnold Stead holds a PhD in English literature (University of
Missouri-Columbia, '93) and is a poet, fiction writer, historian,
playwright, and jazz and film critic. He lives in Minneapolis with
his wife and family.